AUTHENTIC TRANSCRIPTIONS
WITH NOTES AND TABLATURE

PAT MARTINO
GUITAR ANTHOLOGY

Cover photo © R. Andrew Lepley

Music transcriptions by Mike Butzen and Paul Pappas

ISBN 978-1-4950-0575-6

HAL•LEONARD®
CORPORATION

7777 W. BLUEMOUND RD. P.O. BOX 13819 MILWAUKEE, WI 53213

from *Footprints*

Alone Together

Lyrics by Howard Dietz
Music by Arthur Schwartz

*Chord symbols reflect overall harmony.

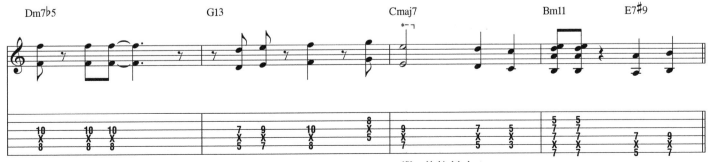

*Played behind the beat.

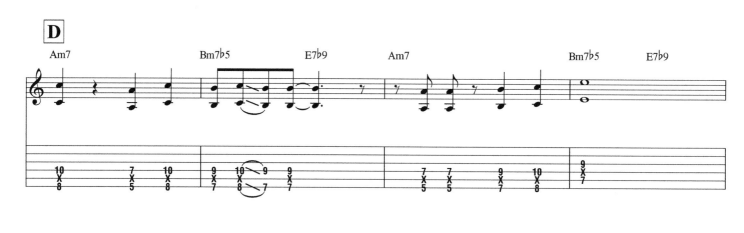

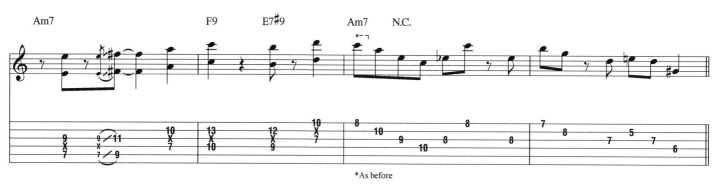

*As before

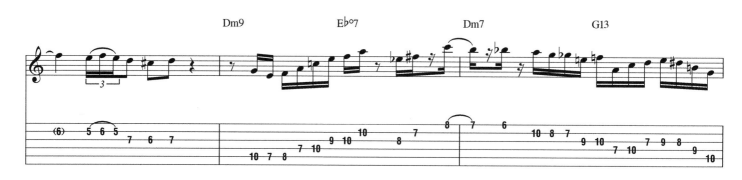

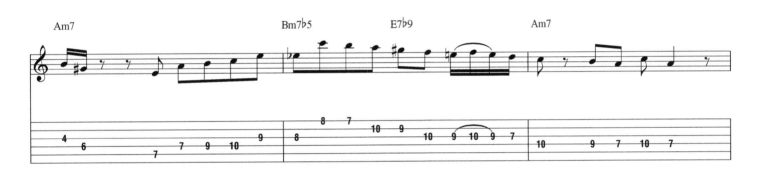

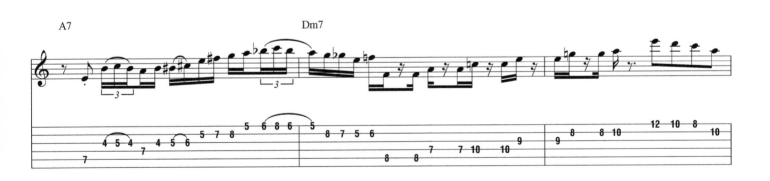

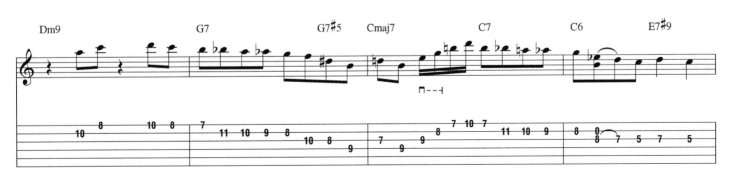

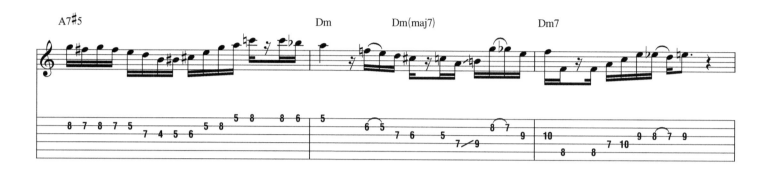

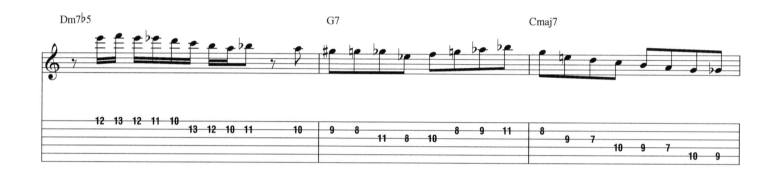

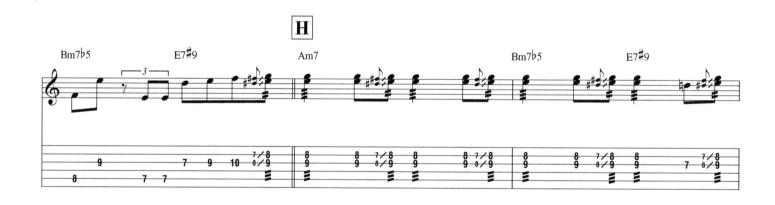

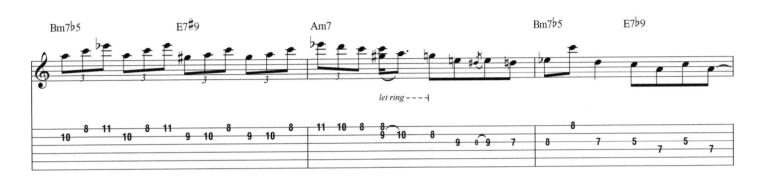

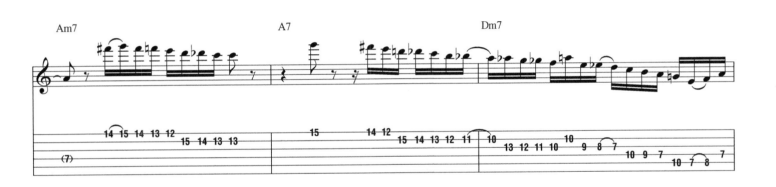

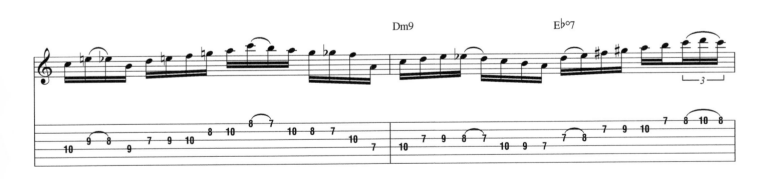

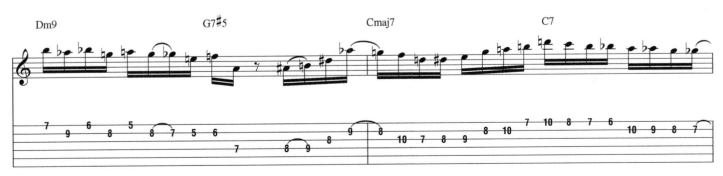

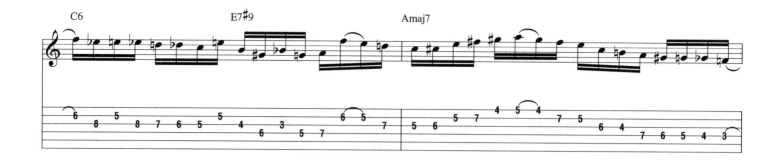

J

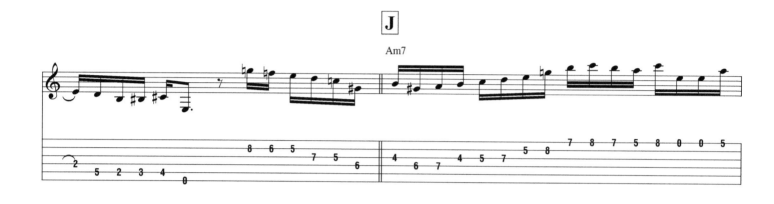

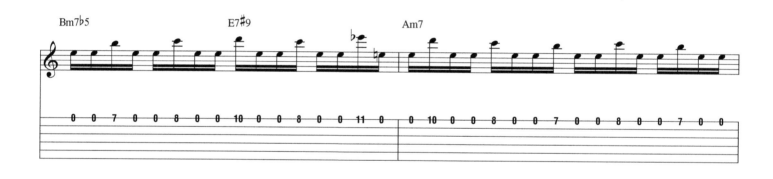

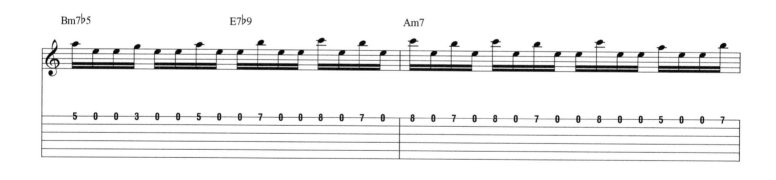

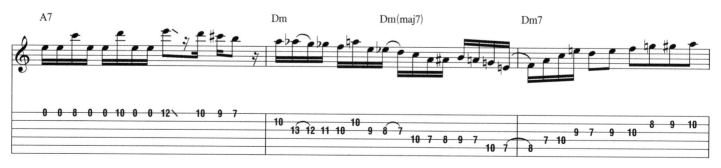

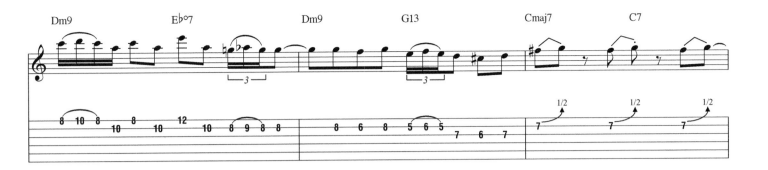

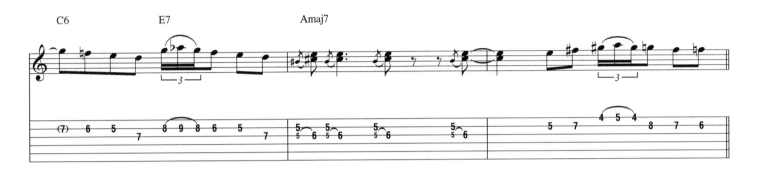

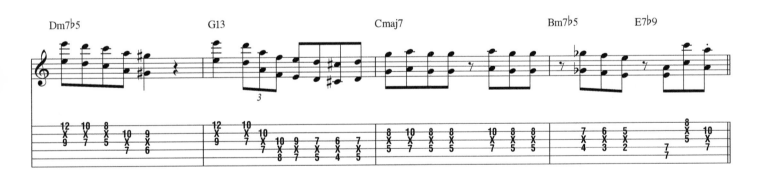

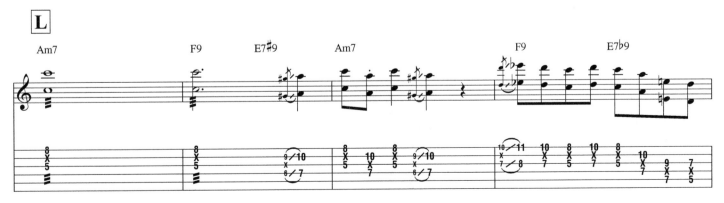

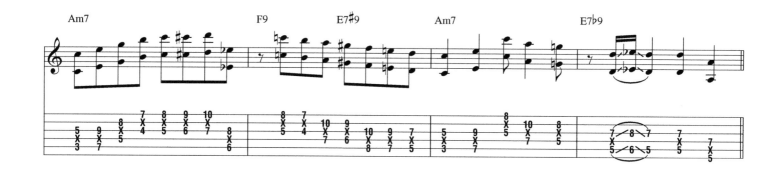

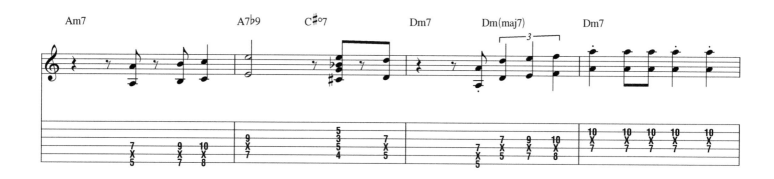

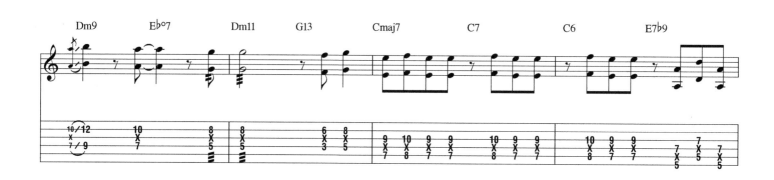

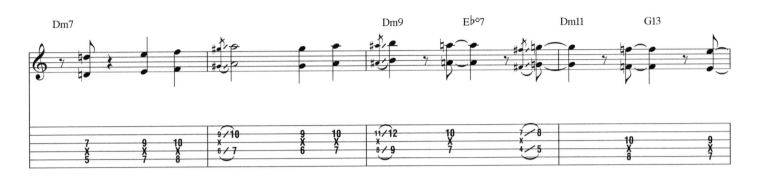

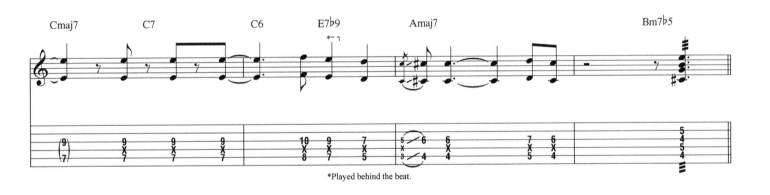

*Played behind the beat.

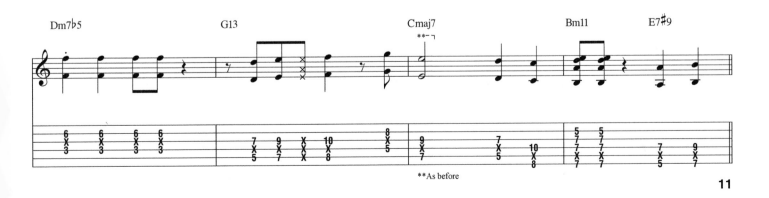

**As before

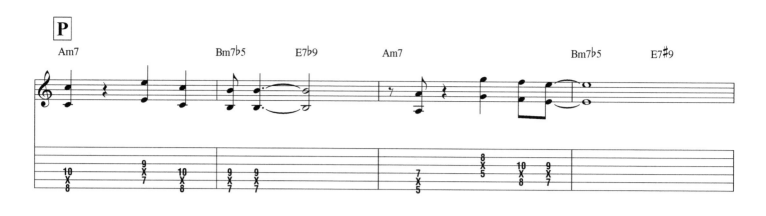

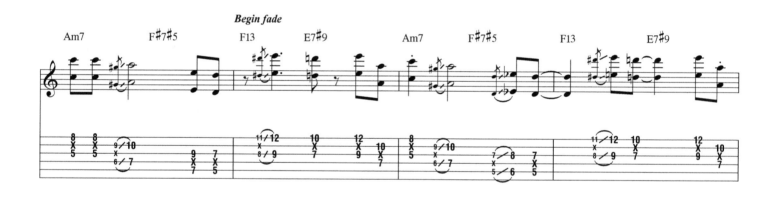

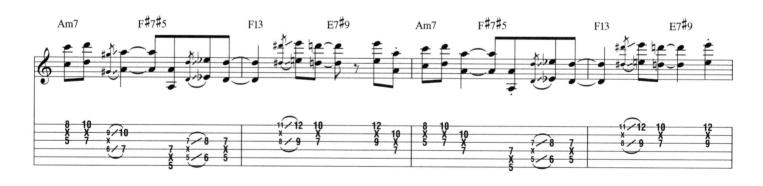

from *Consciousness*
Both Sides Now
Words and Music by Joni Mitchell

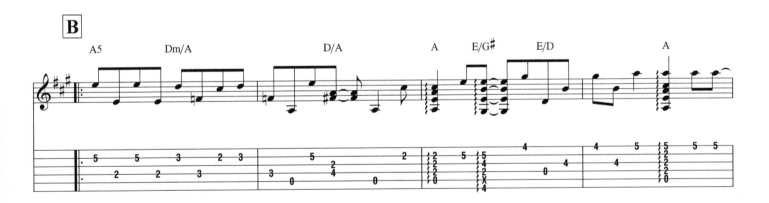

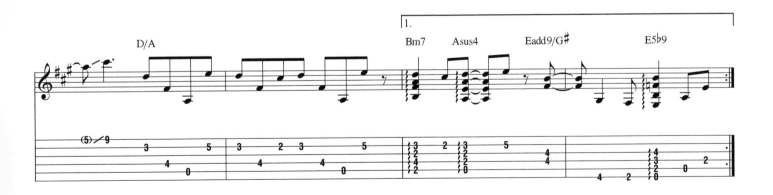

Catch

By Pat Martino

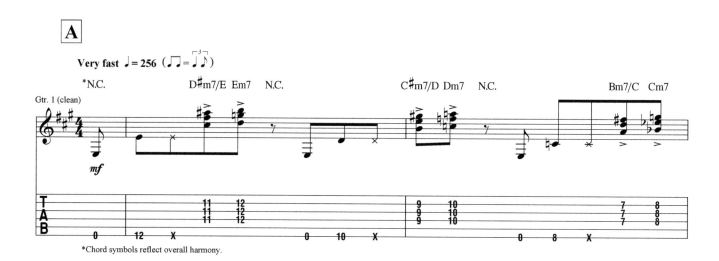

*Chord symbols reflect overall harmony.

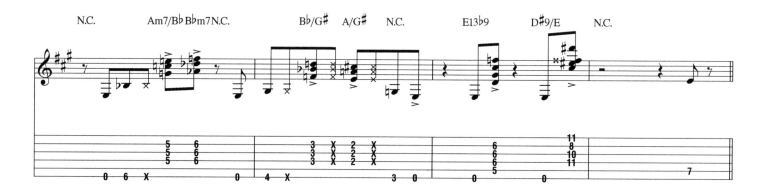

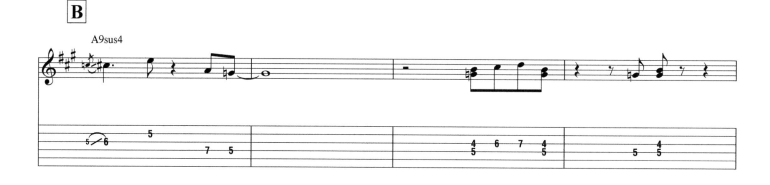

A9sus4

D9

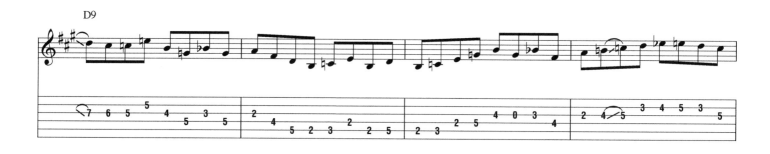

B9

C#9

A9sus4

D9

D

A9sus4

D9

A9sus4

A9sus4

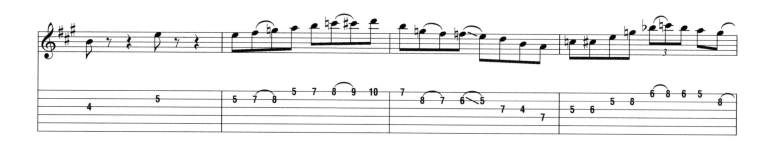

D9

A6

A6

E   **F**   **G**

A6   A9sus4

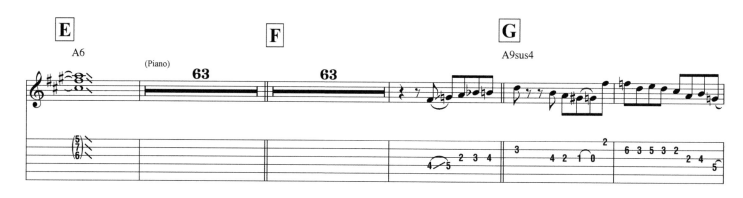

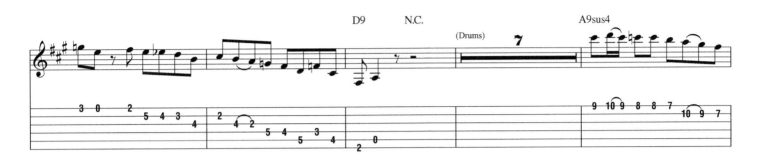

from *East*
Close Your Eyes
By Bernice Petkere

B

*Chord symbols reflect overall harmony.

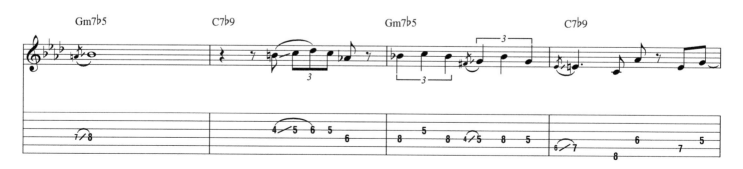

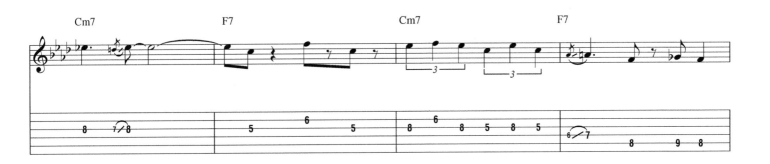

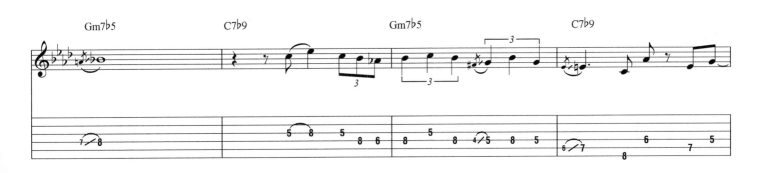

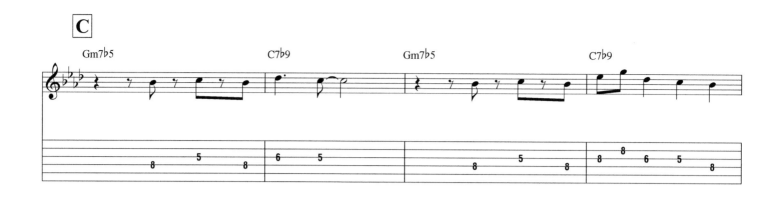

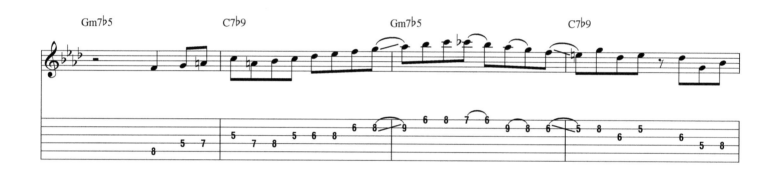

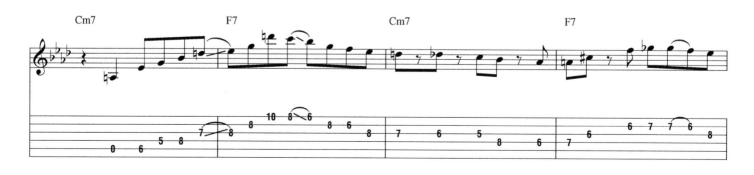

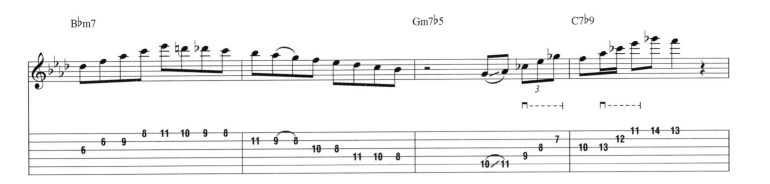

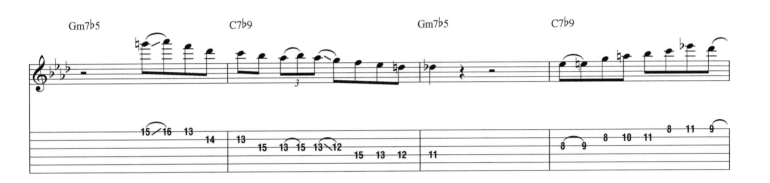

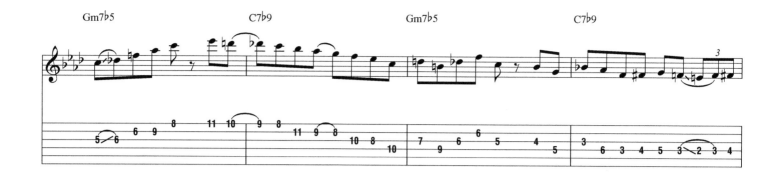

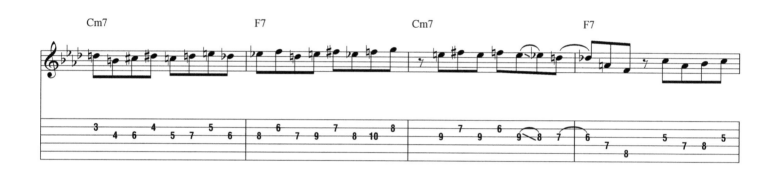

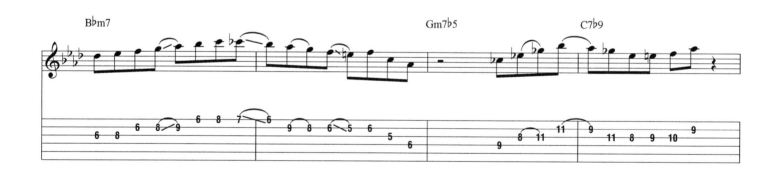

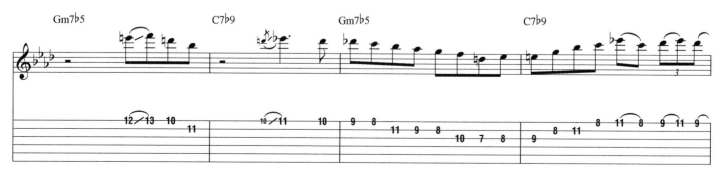

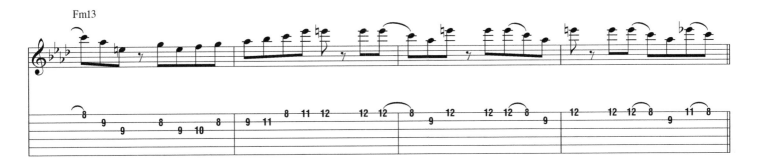

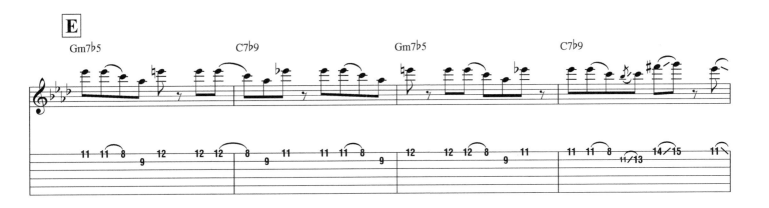

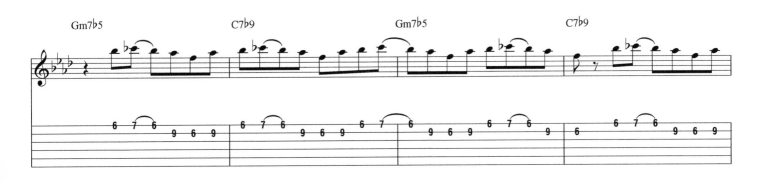

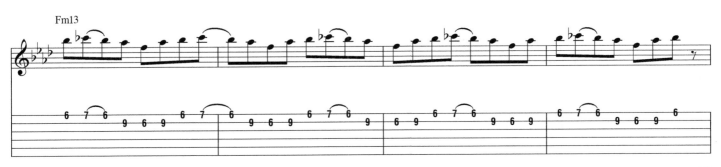

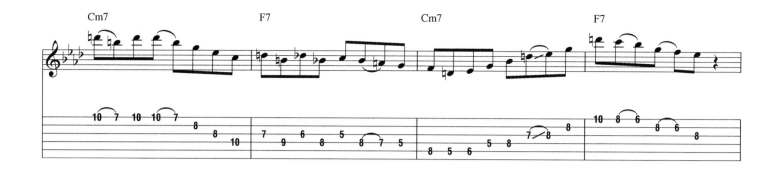

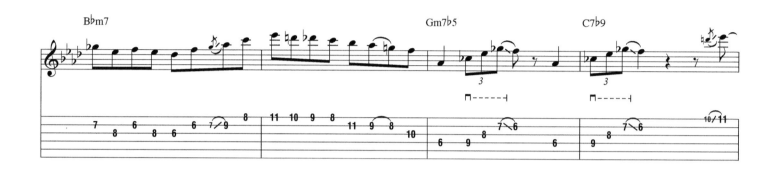

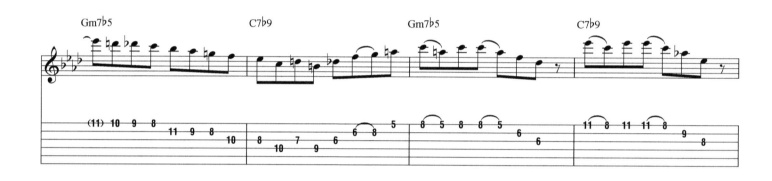

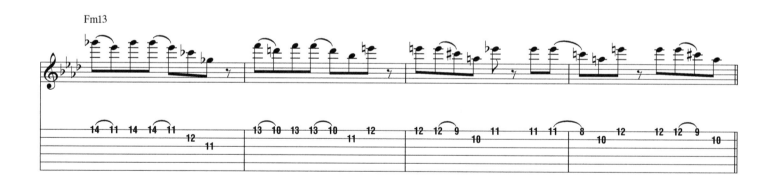

F

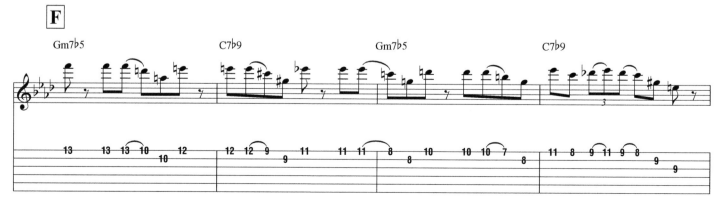

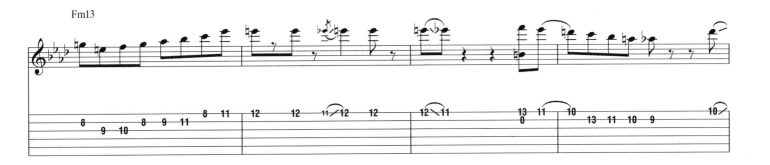

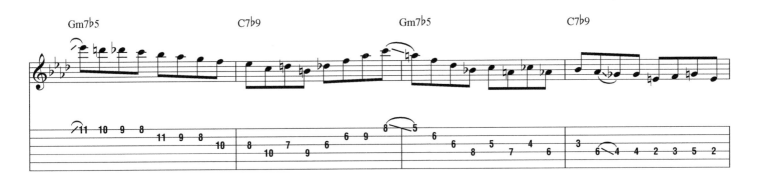

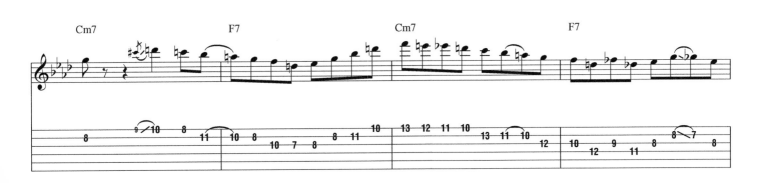

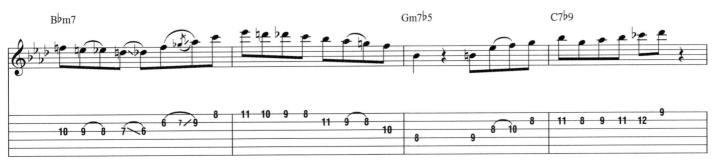

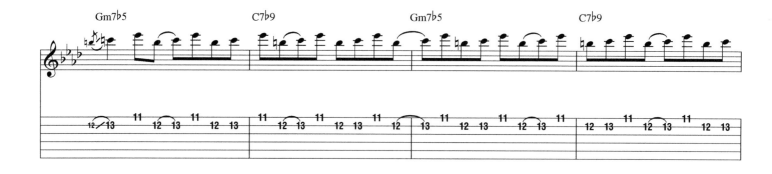

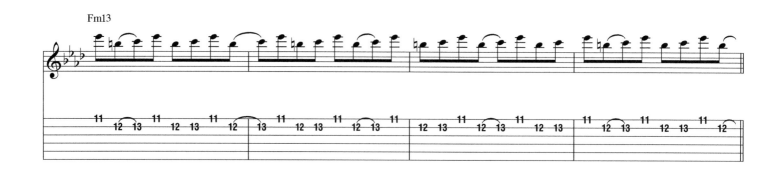

G

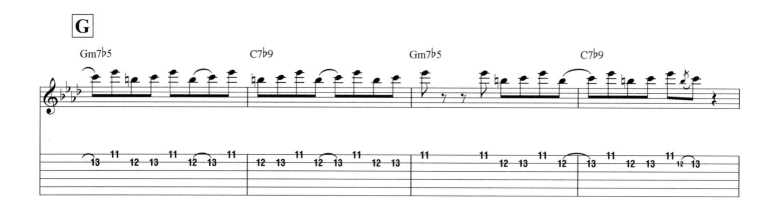

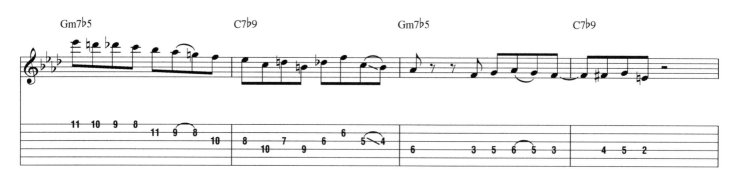

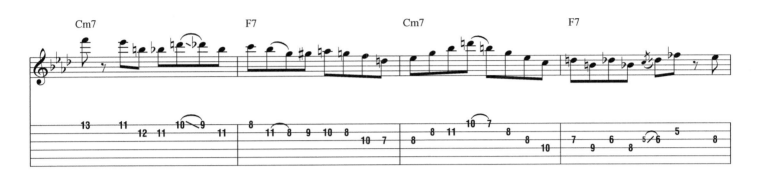

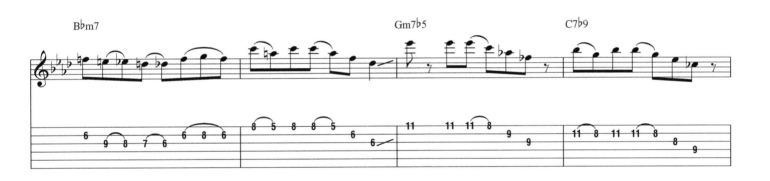

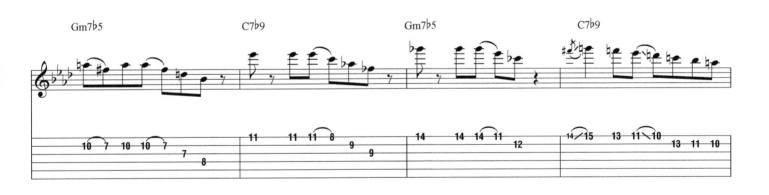

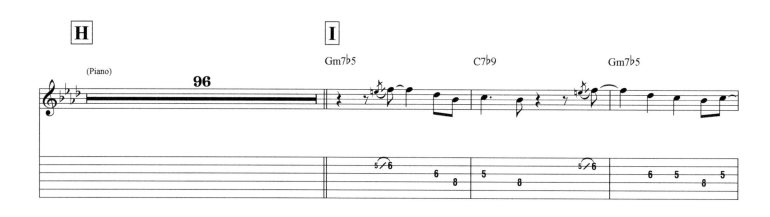

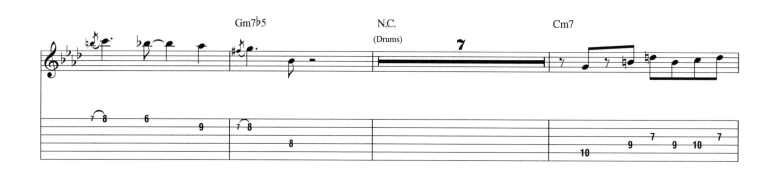

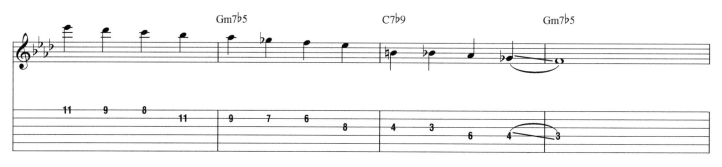

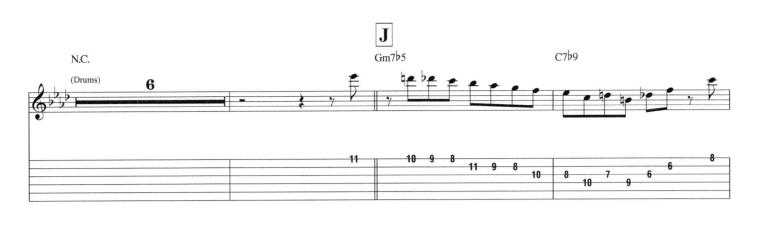

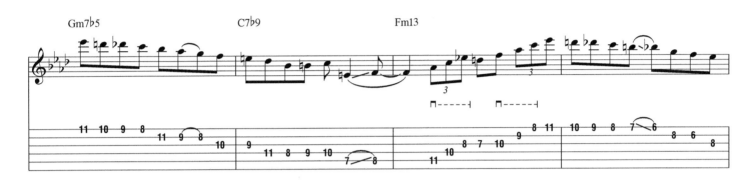

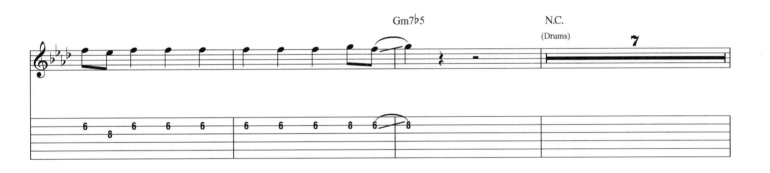

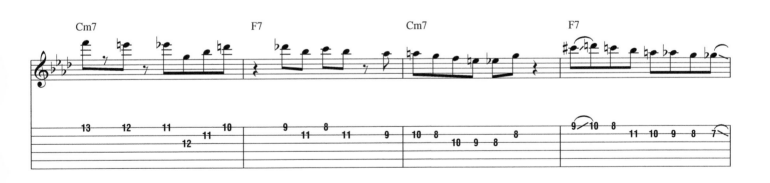

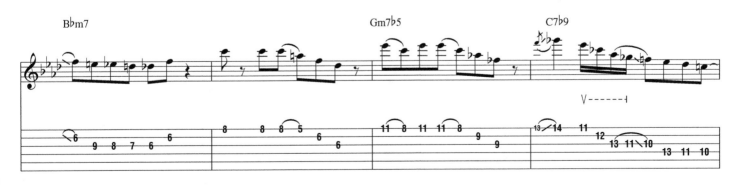

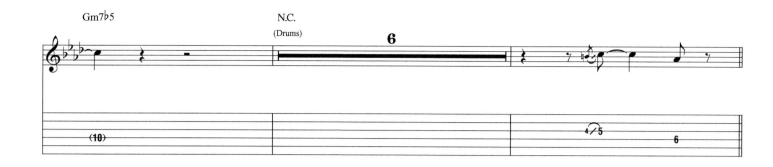

K

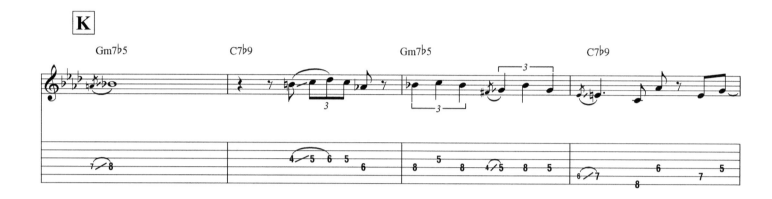

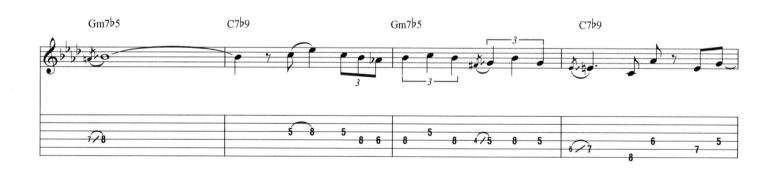

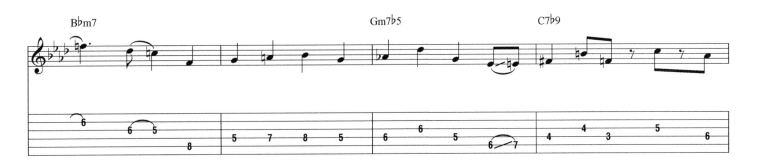

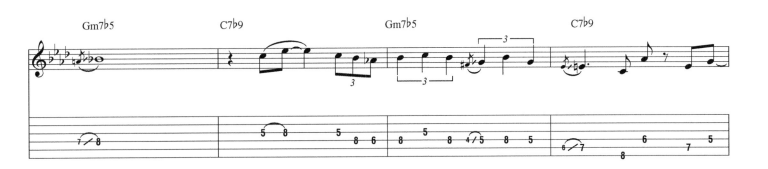

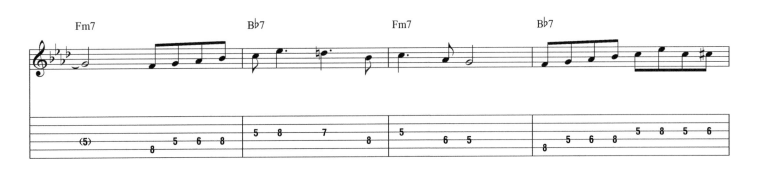

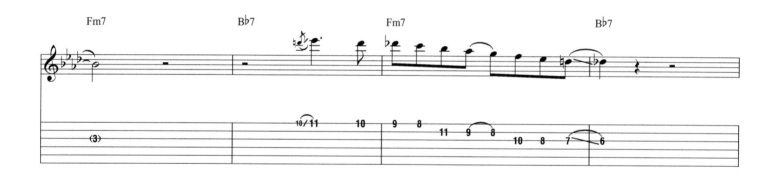

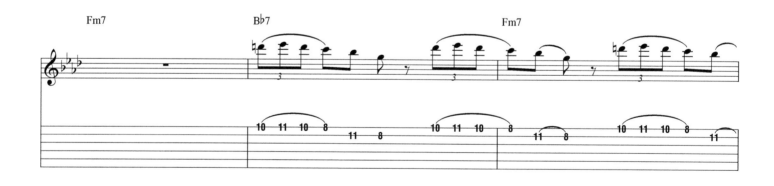

from *Footprints*

How Insensitive
(Insensatez)

Music by Antonio Carlos Jobim
Original Words by Vinicius de Moraes
English Words by Norman Gimbel

*Chord symbols reflect overall harmony.

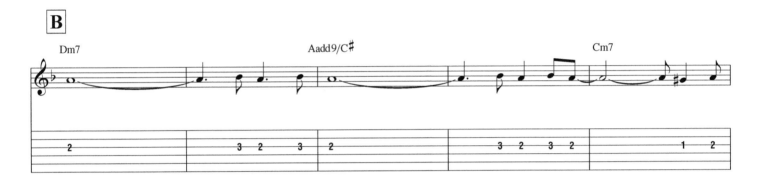

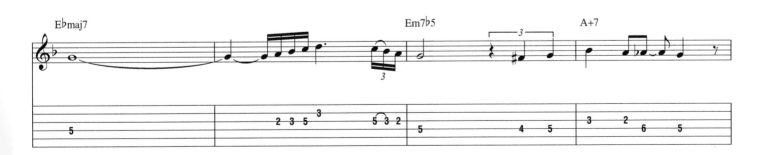

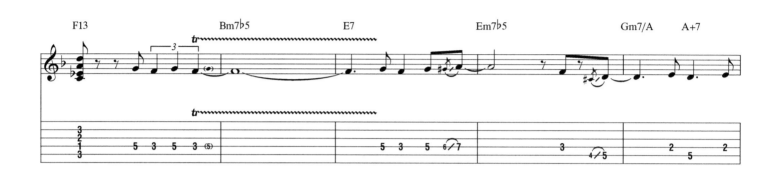

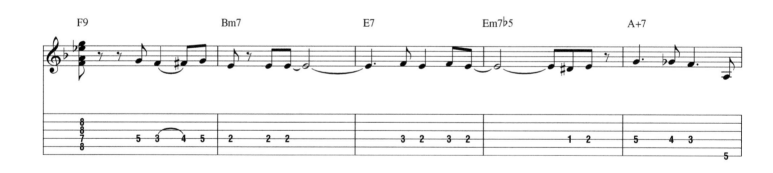

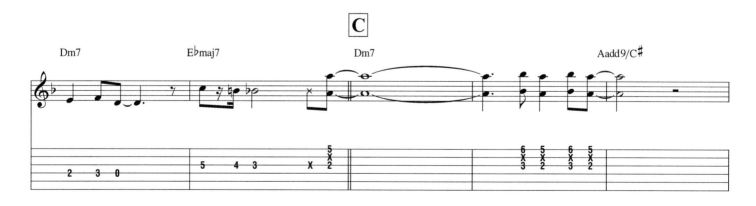

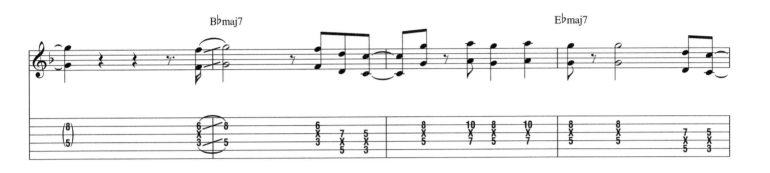

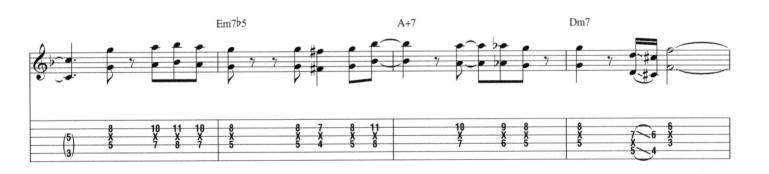

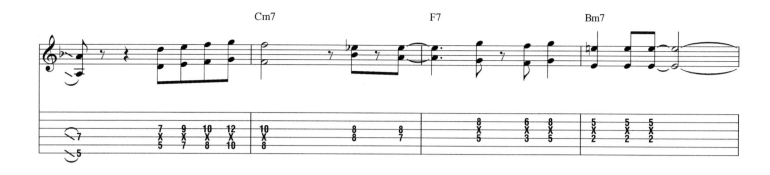

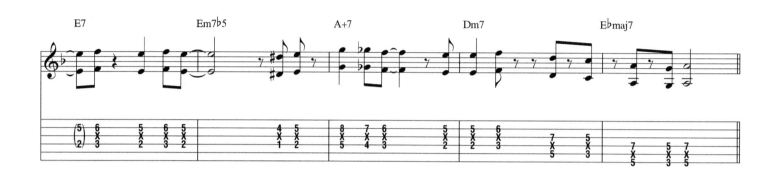

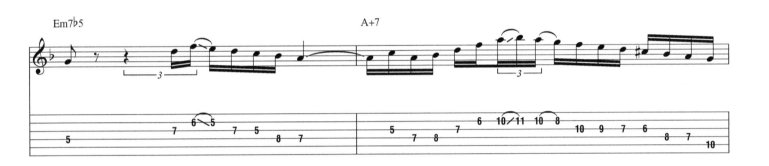

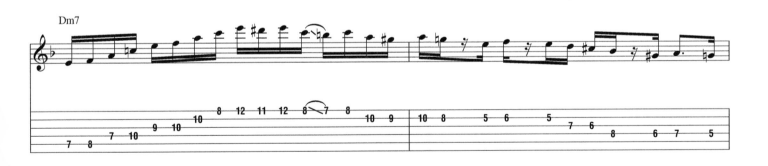

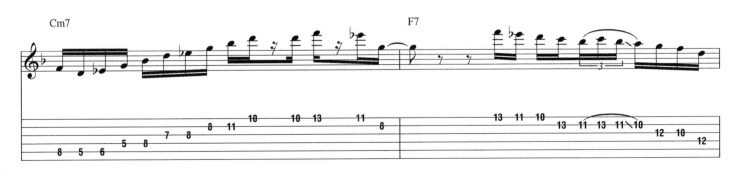

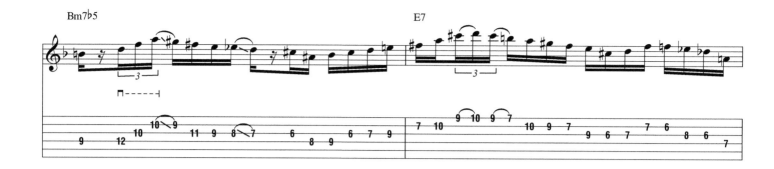

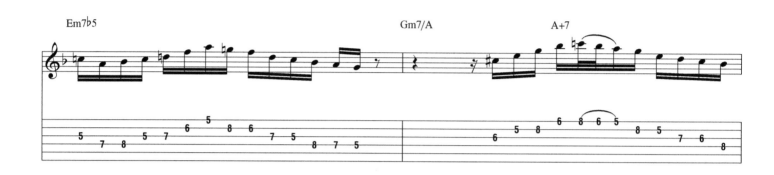

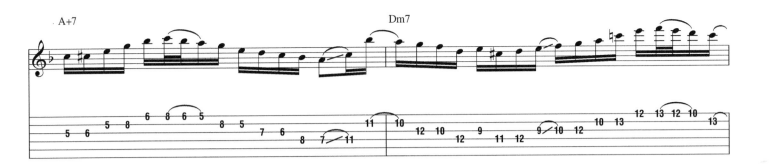

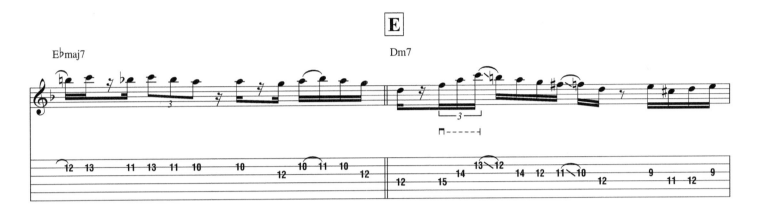

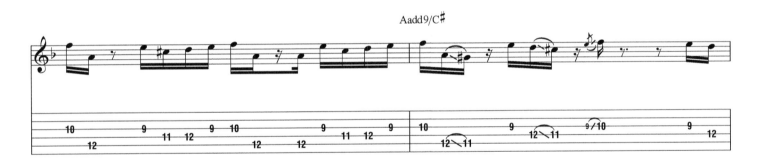

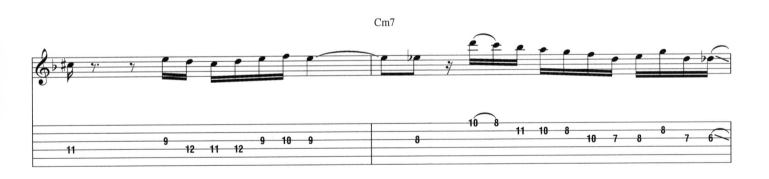

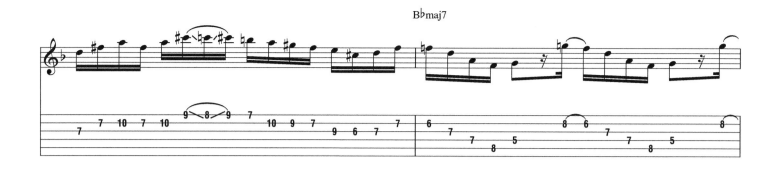

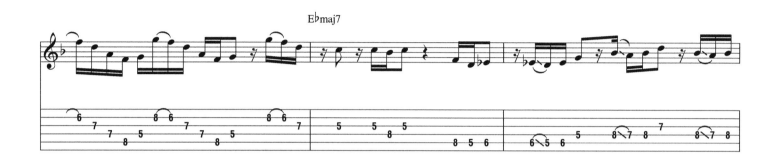

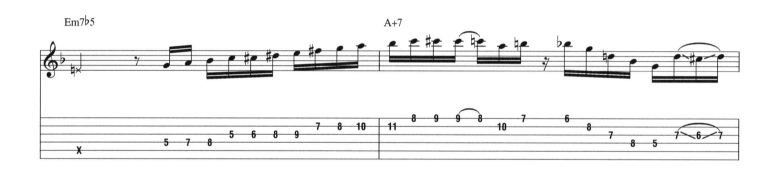

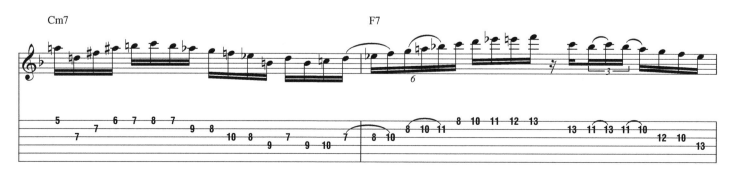

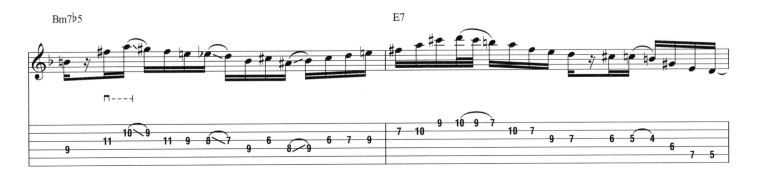

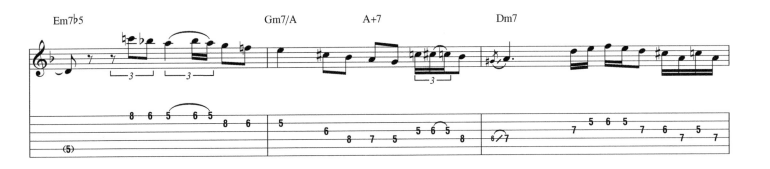

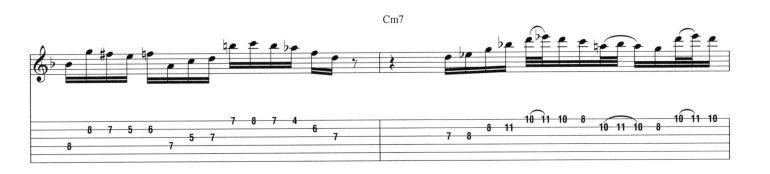

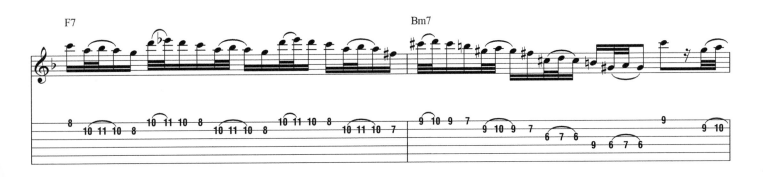

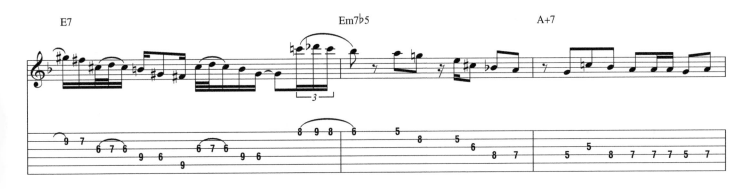

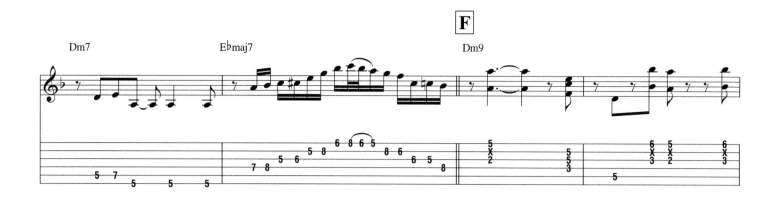

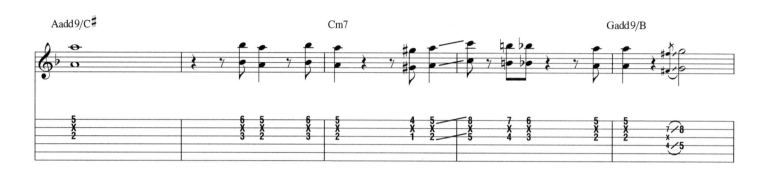

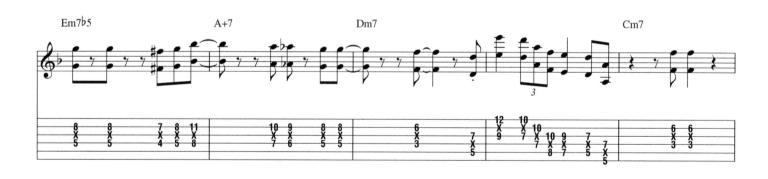

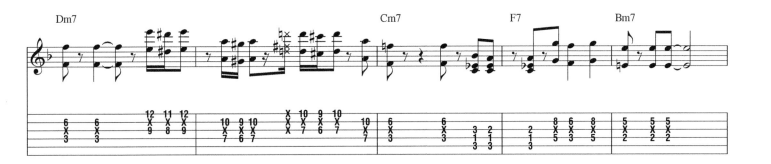

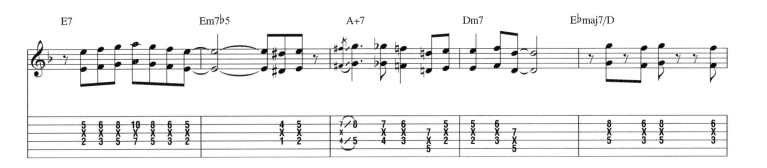

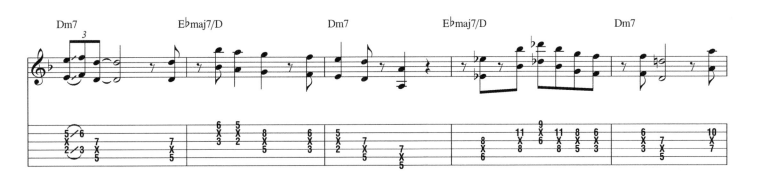

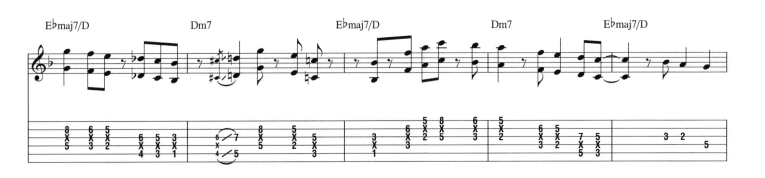

from *Consciousness*
Impressions
By John Coltrane

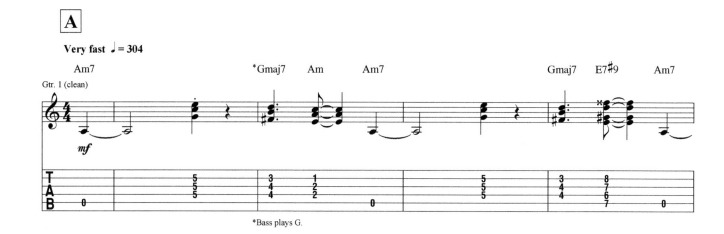

*Bass plays G.

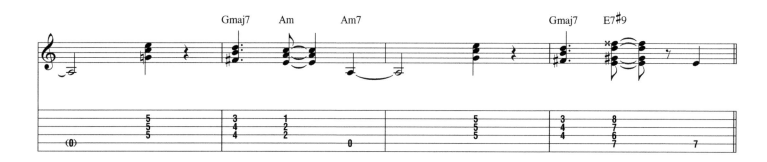

**Chord symbols reflect overall harmony.

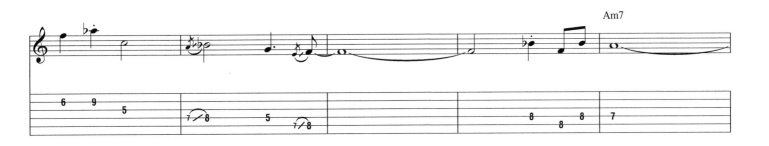

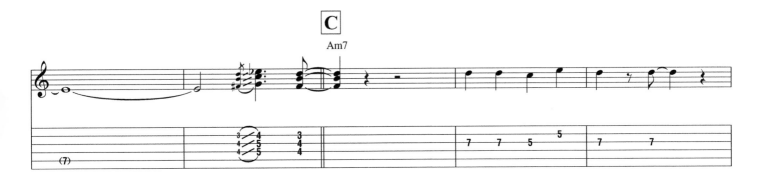

Bbm7

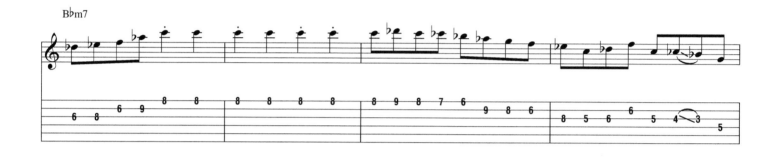

Am7

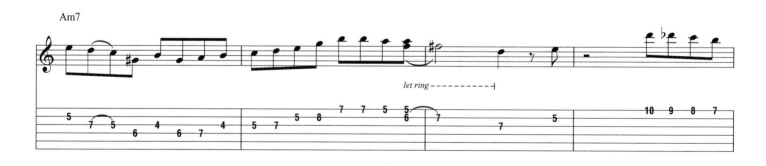

D

59

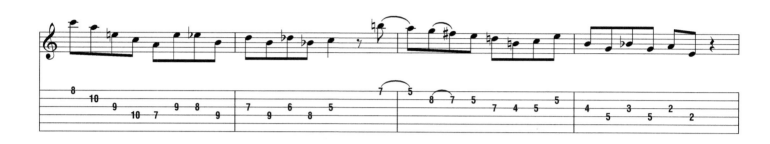

B♭m7

Am7

K

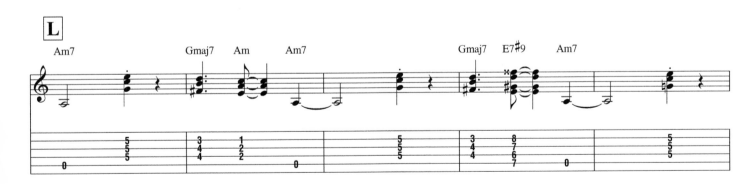

from *El Hombre*

Just Friends

Lyrics by Sam M. Lewis
Music by John Klenner

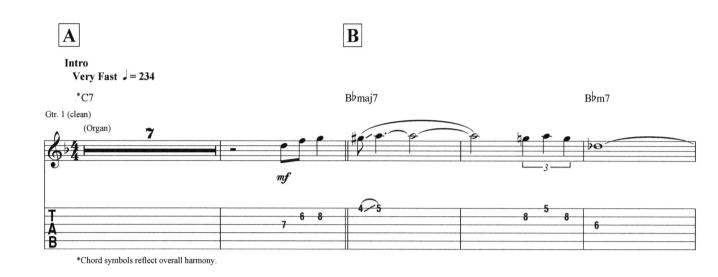

*Chord symbols reflect overall harmony.

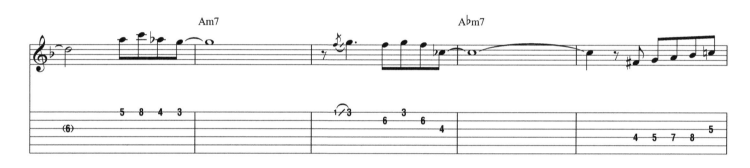

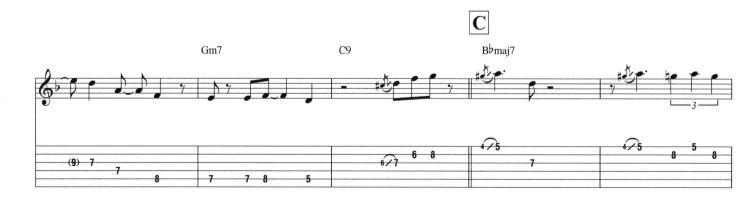

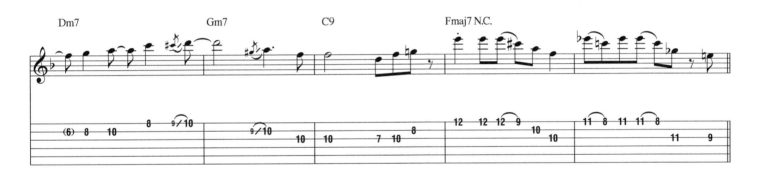

D

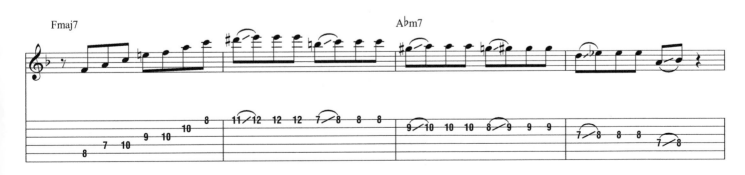

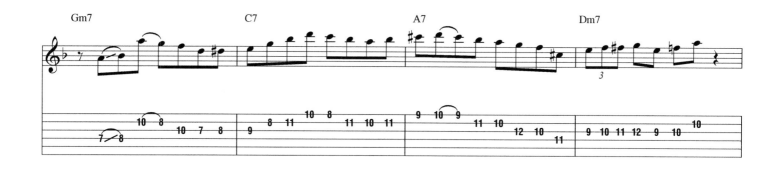

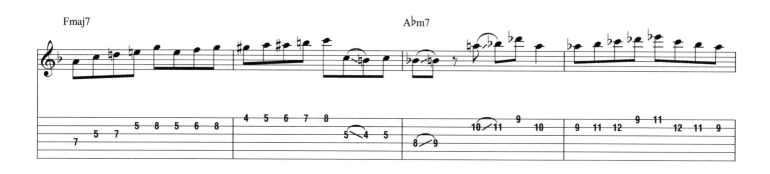

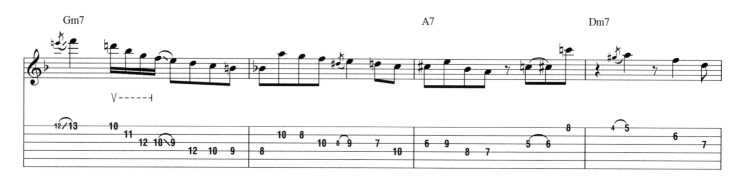

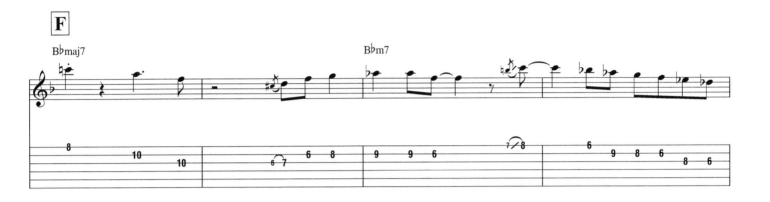

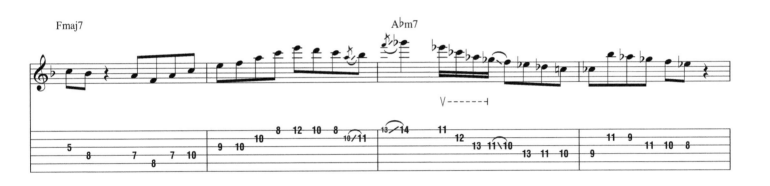

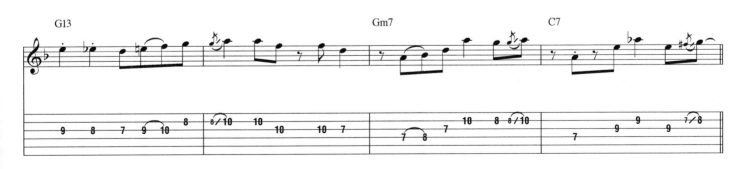

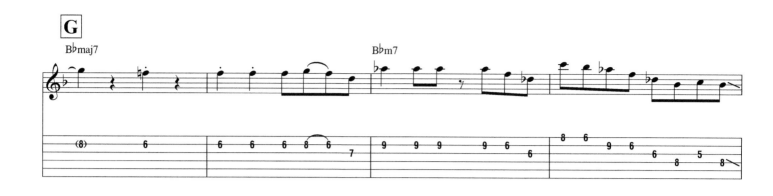

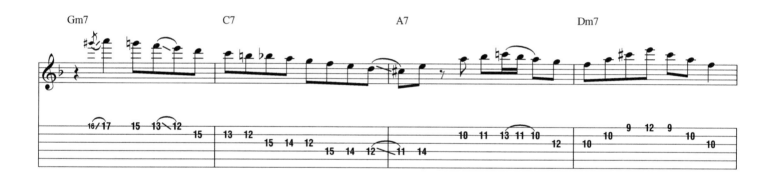

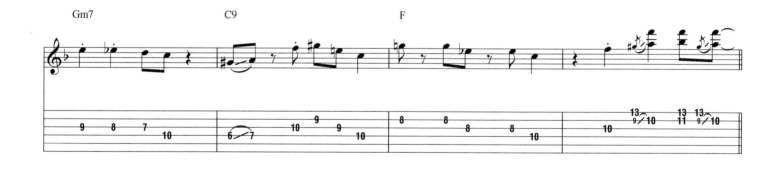

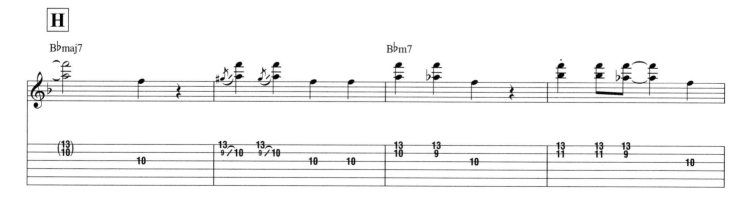

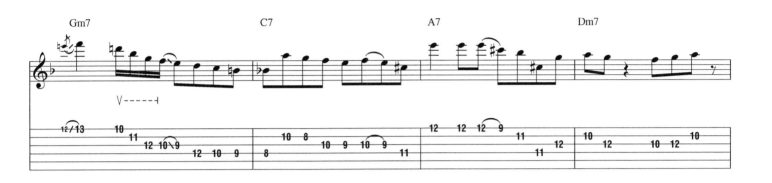

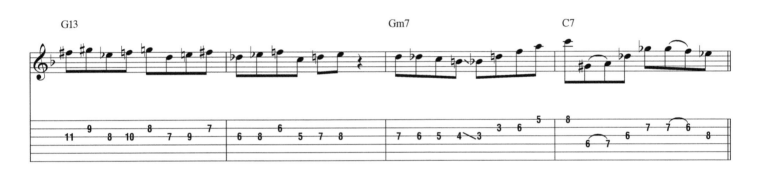

I

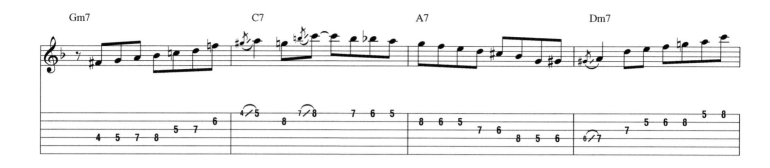

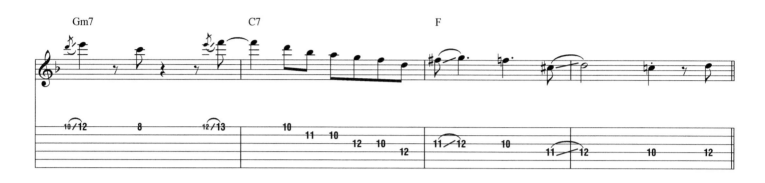

J

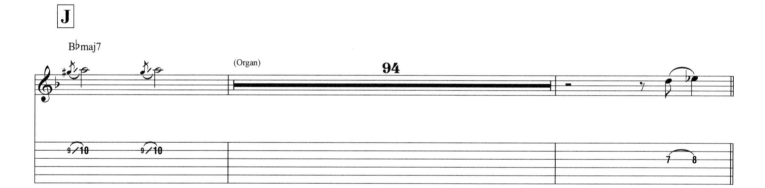

K

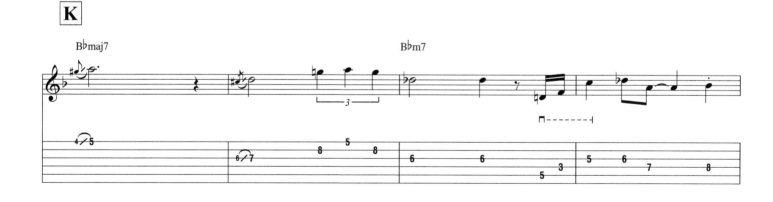

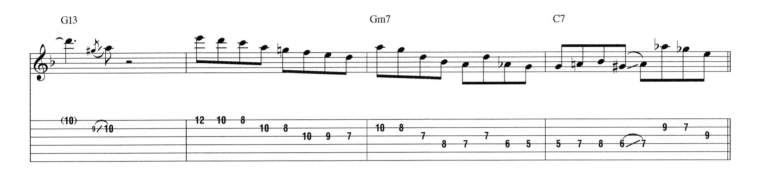

L

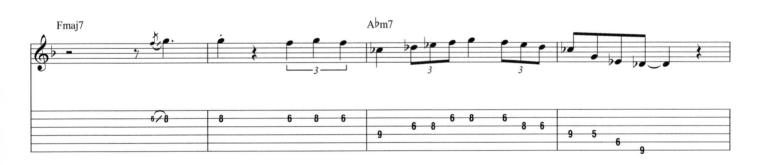

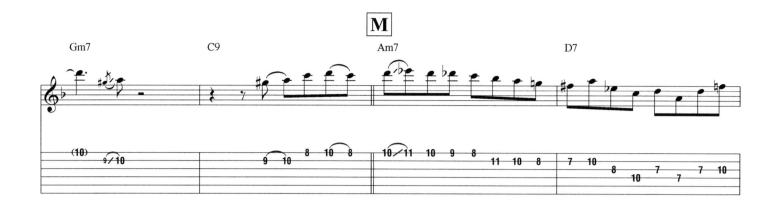

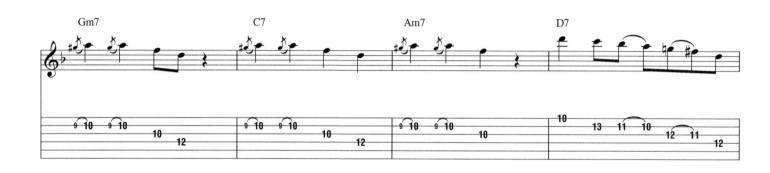

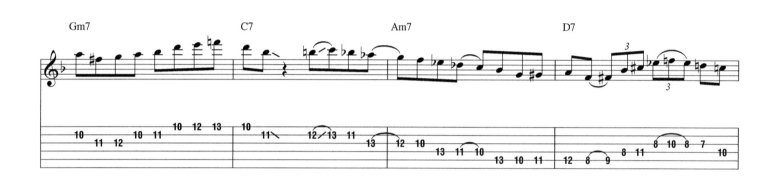

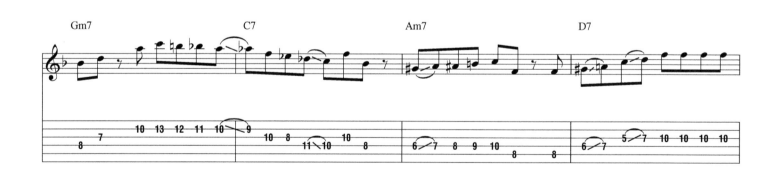

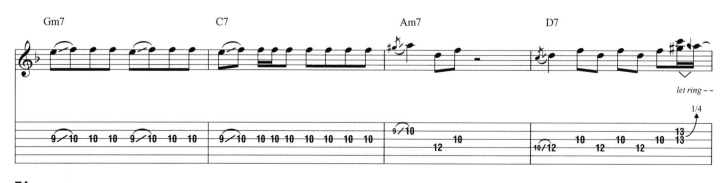

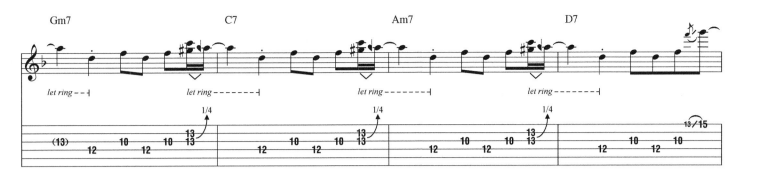

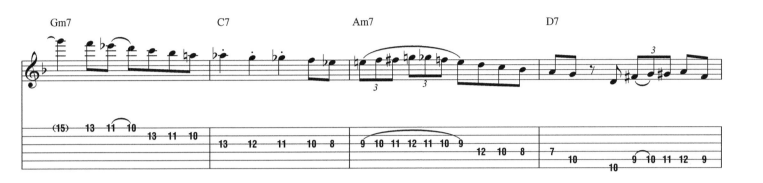

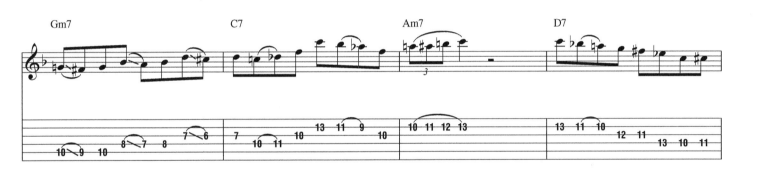

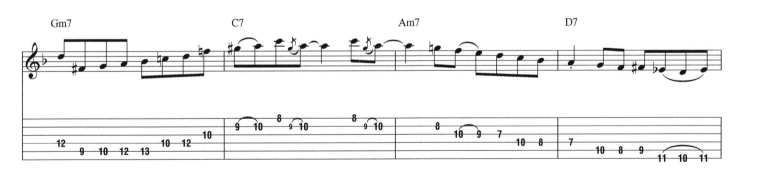

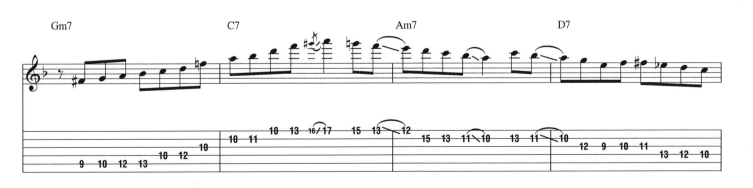

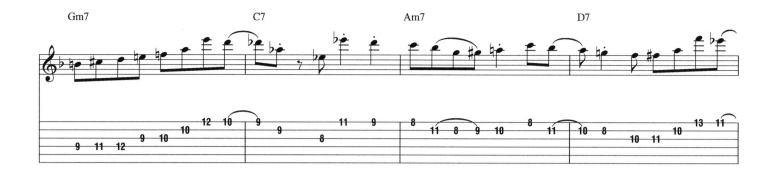

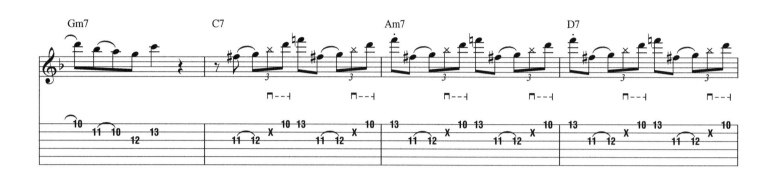

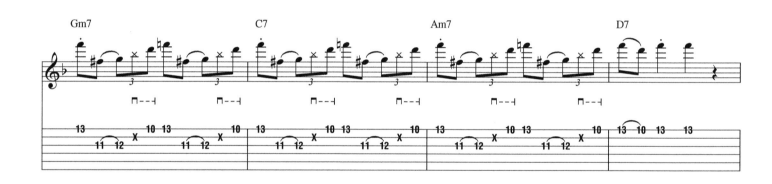

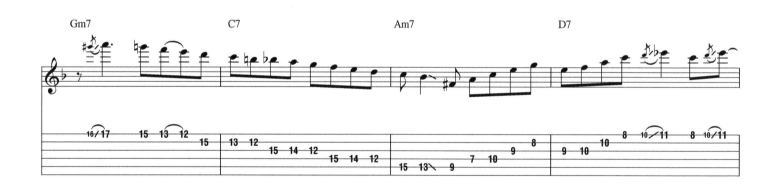

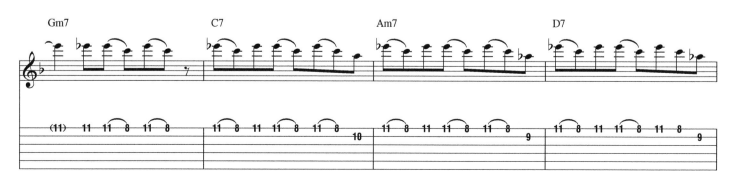

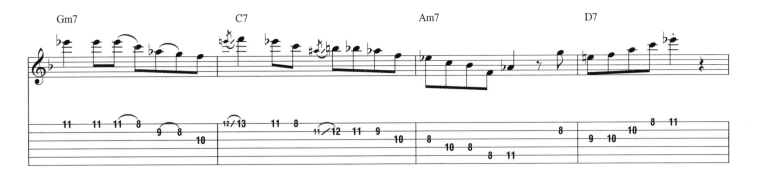

Begin fade

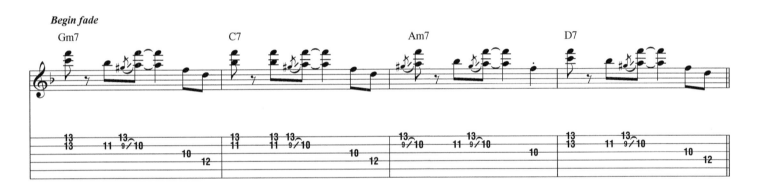

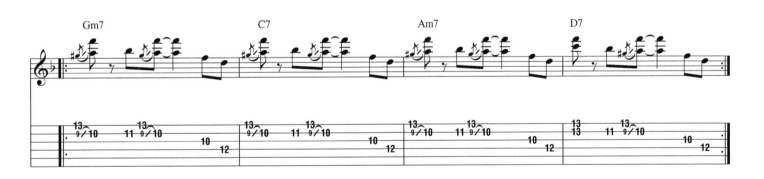

Fade out

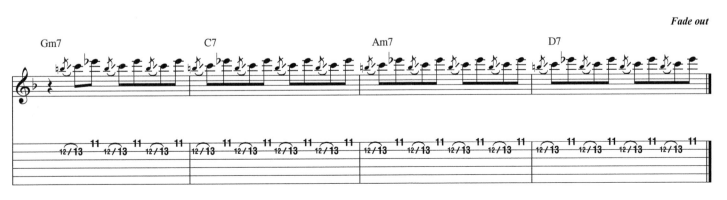

from *East*
Lazy Bird

By John Coltrane

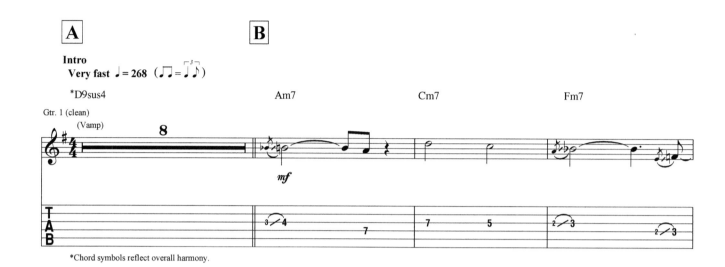

*Chord symbols reflect overall harmony.

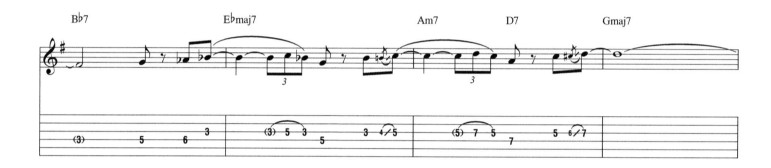

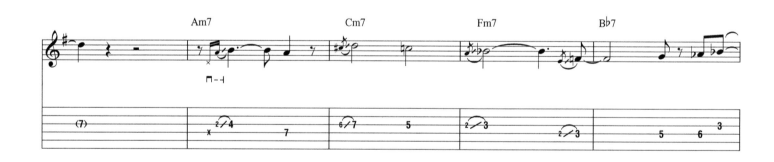

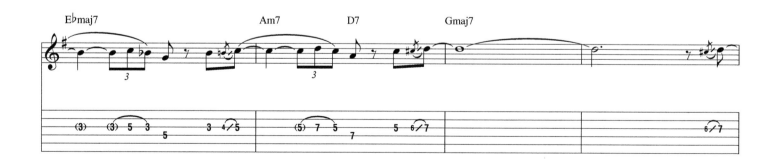

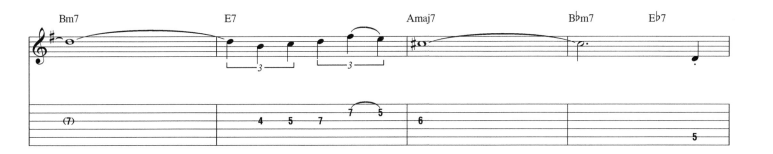

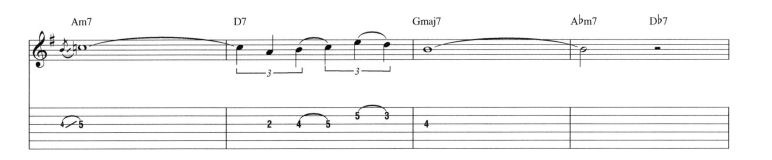

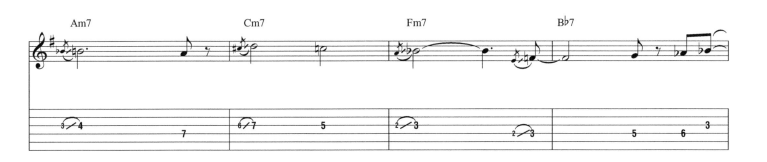

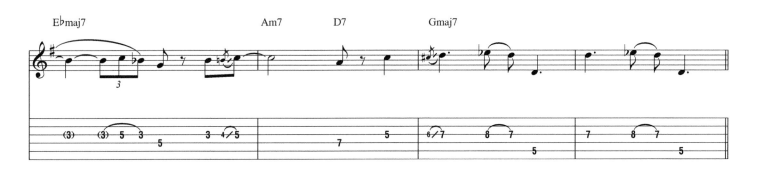

C

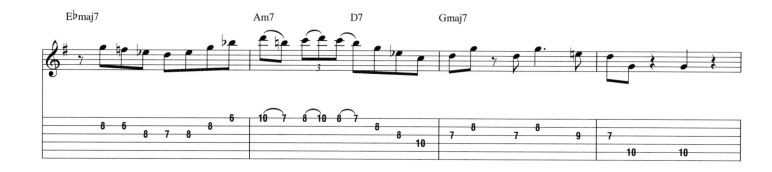

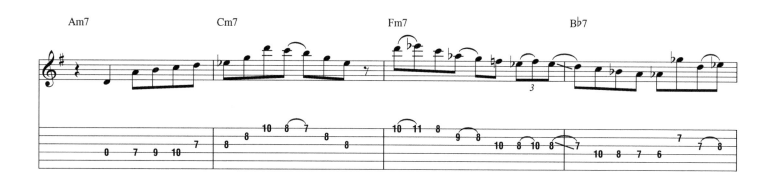

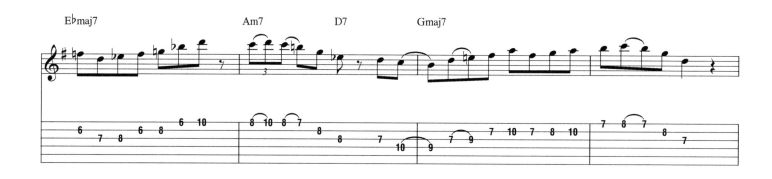

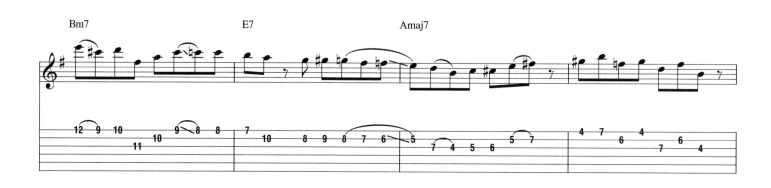

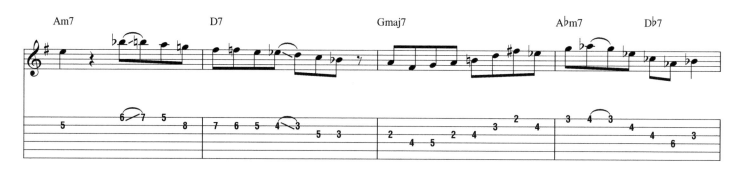

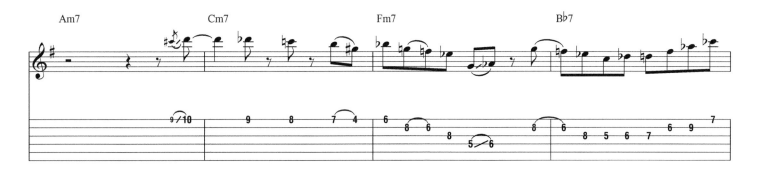

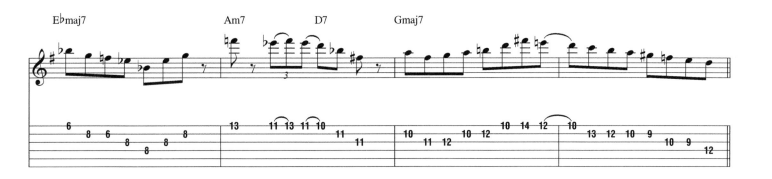

D

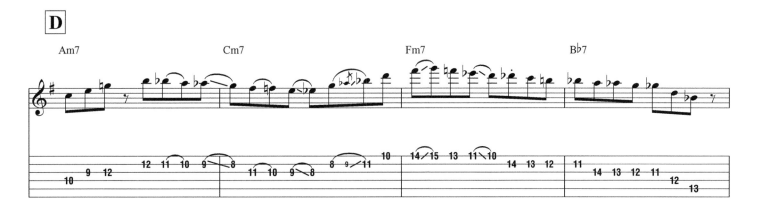

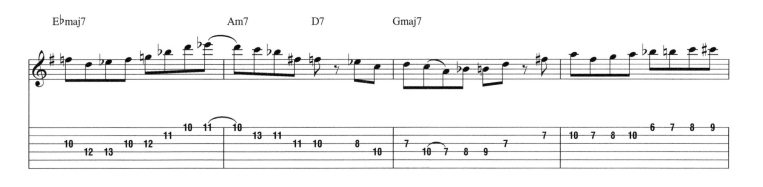

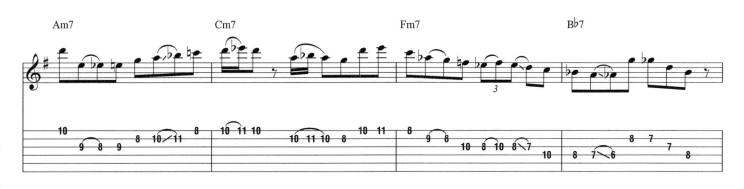

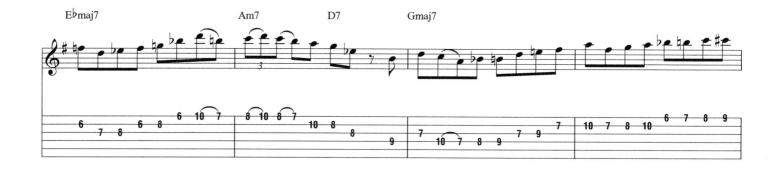

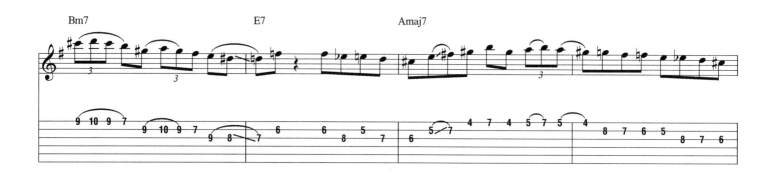

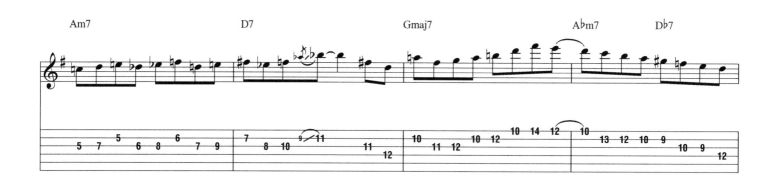

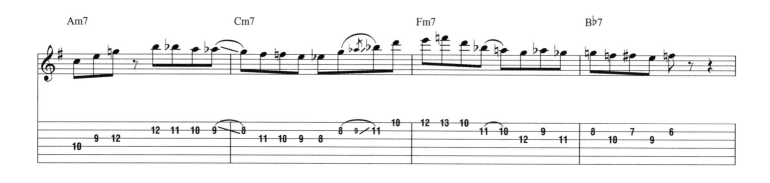

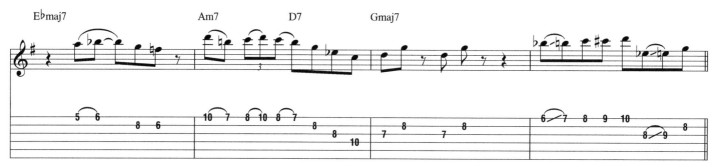

E

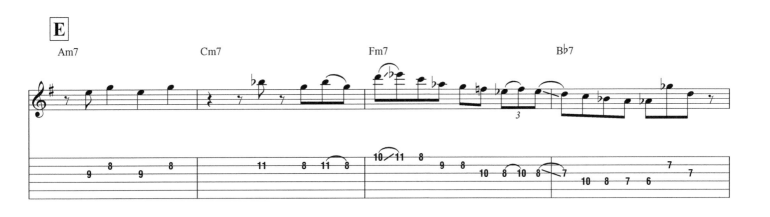

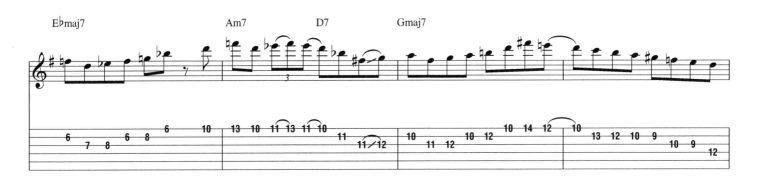

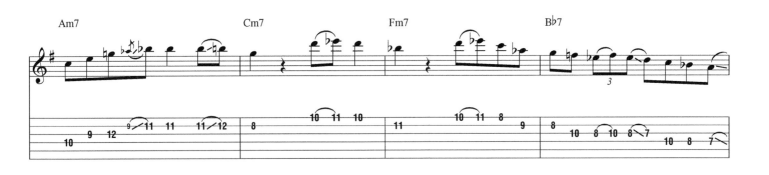

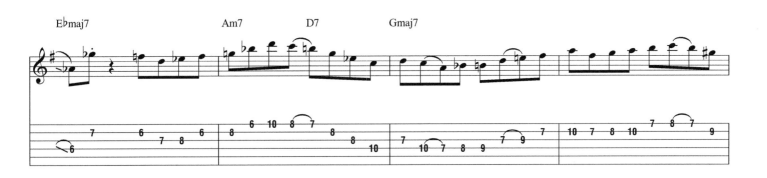

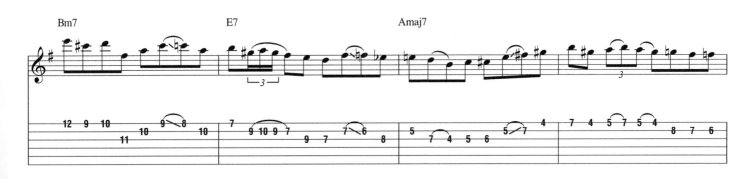

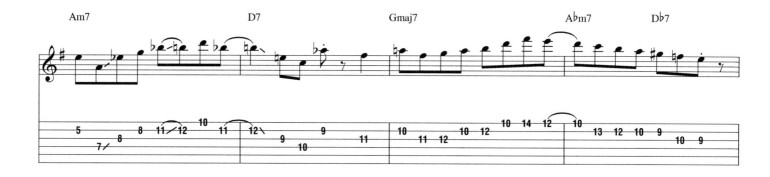

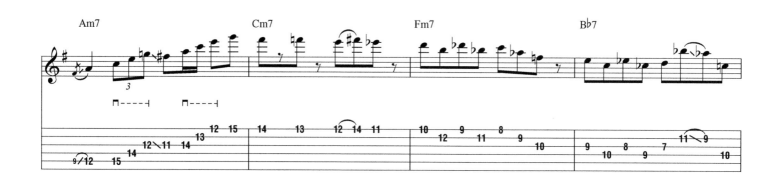

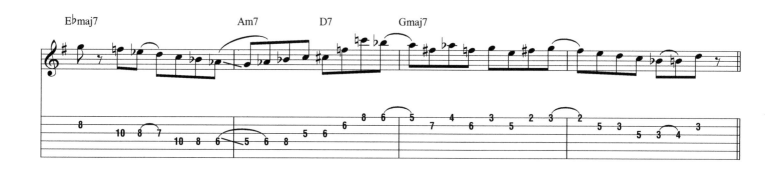

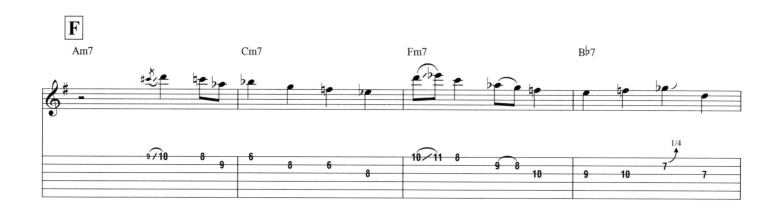

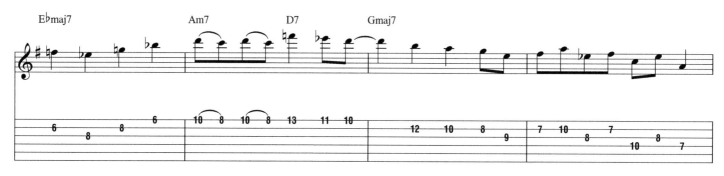

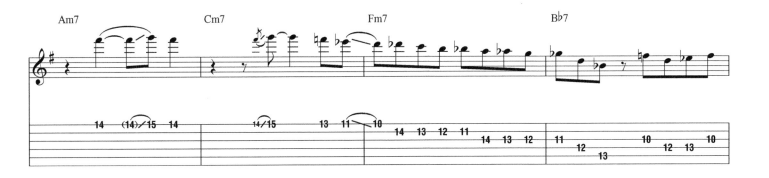

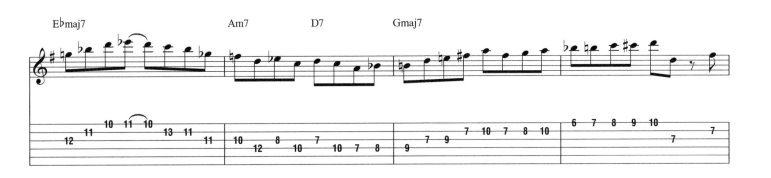

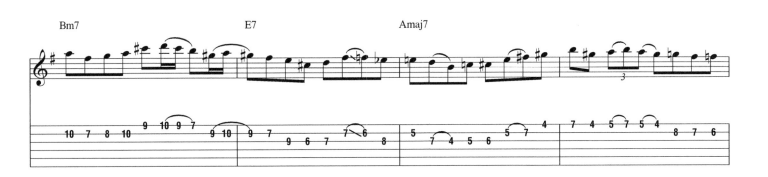

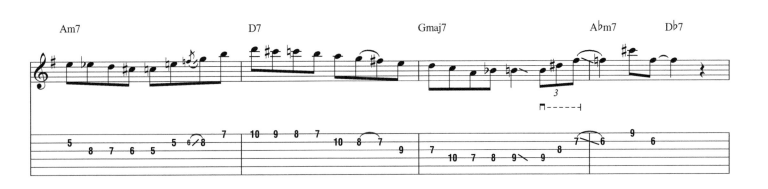

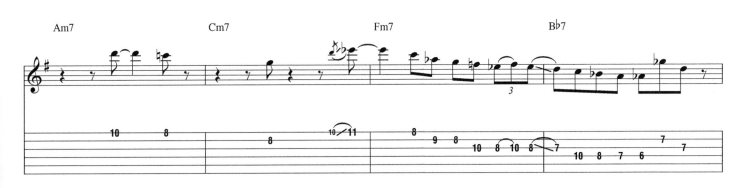

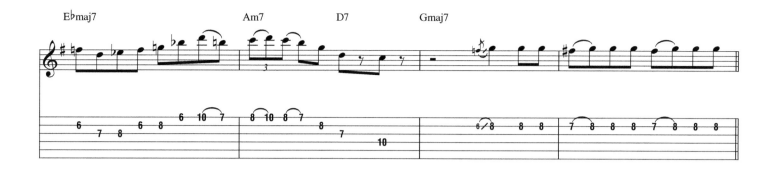

G

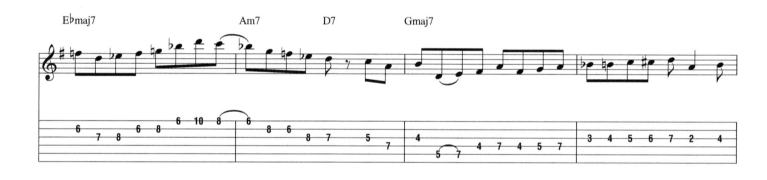

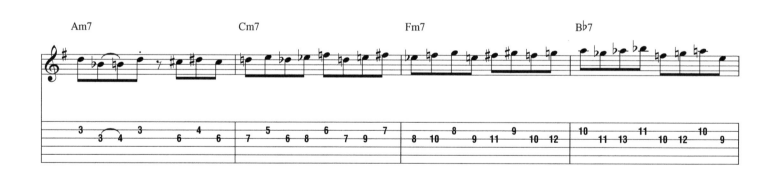

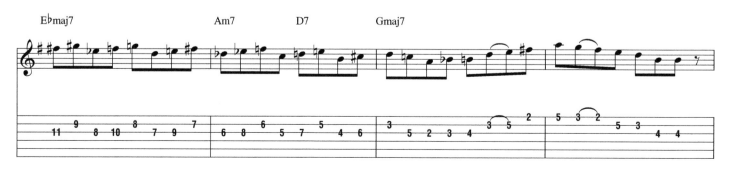

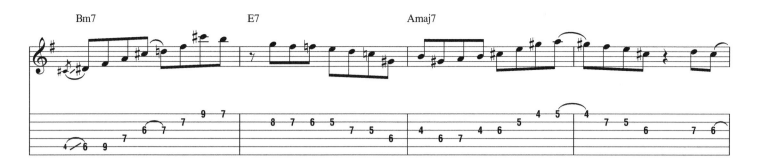

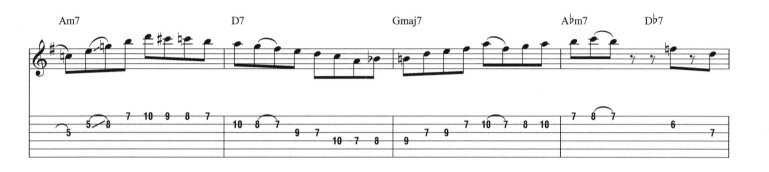

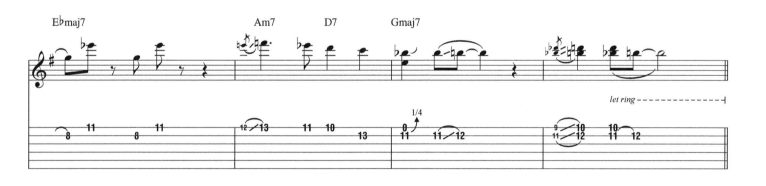

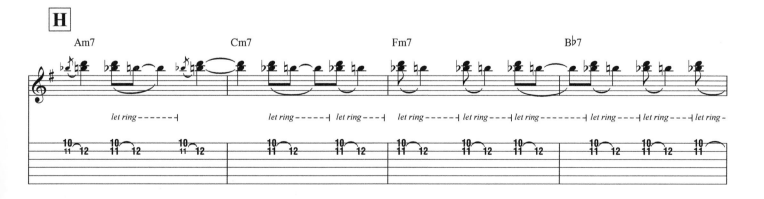

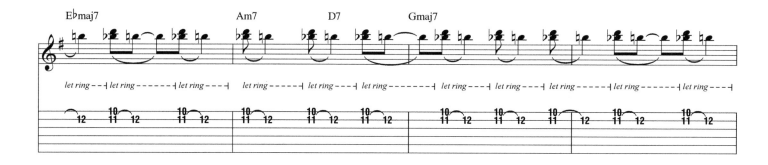

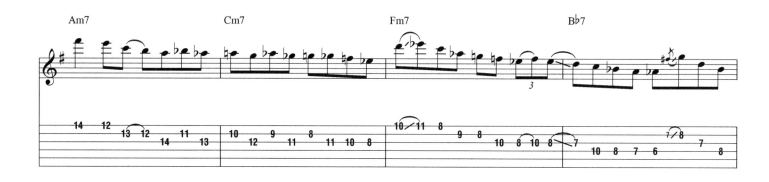

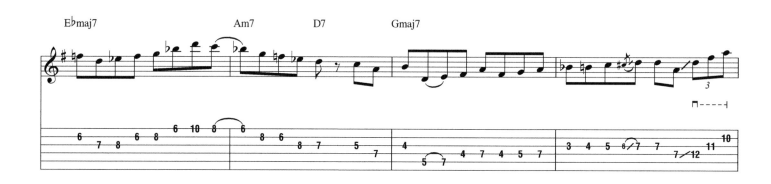

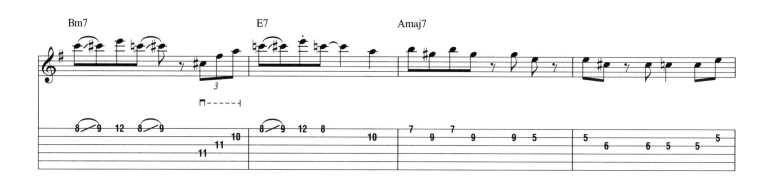

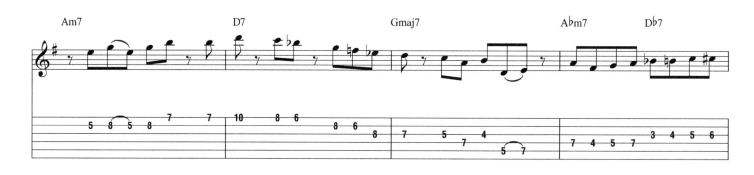

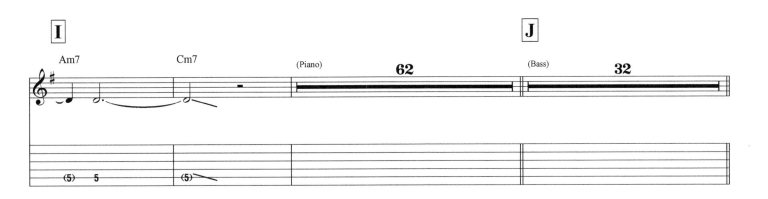

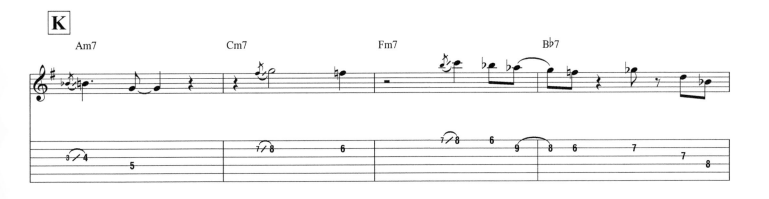

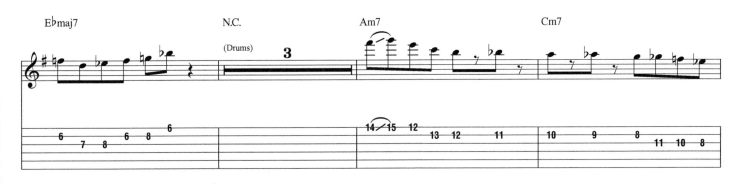

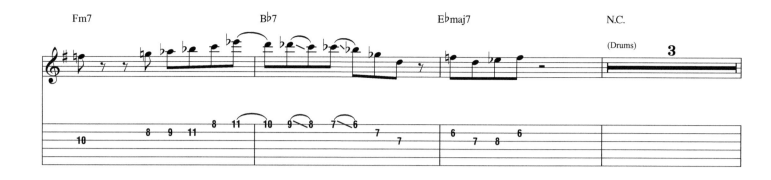

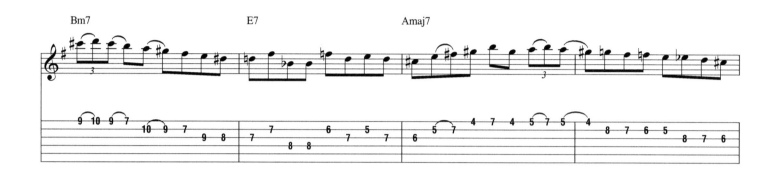

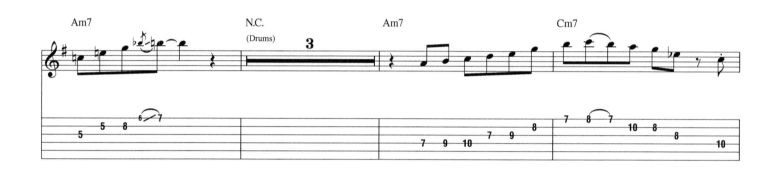

L

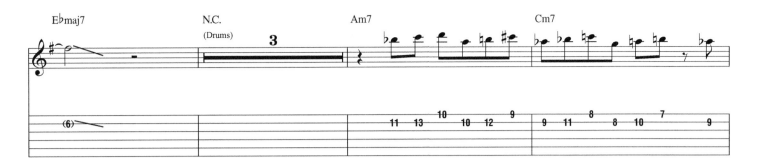
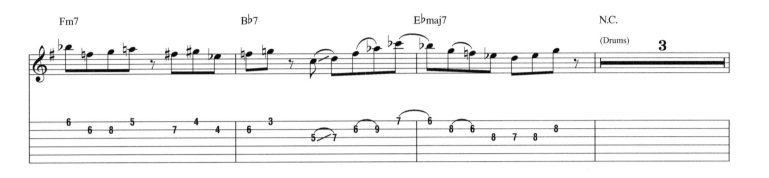
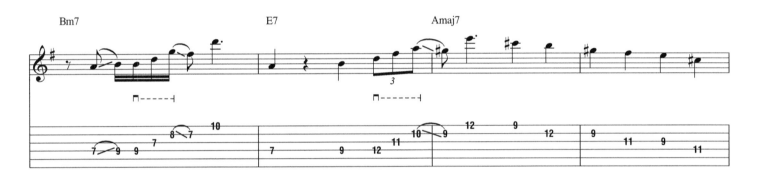
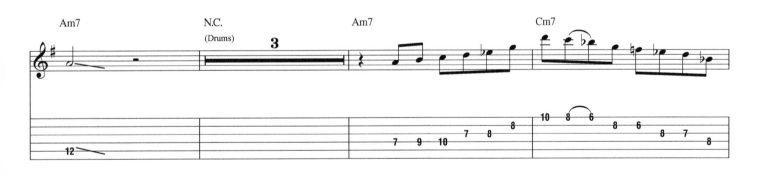
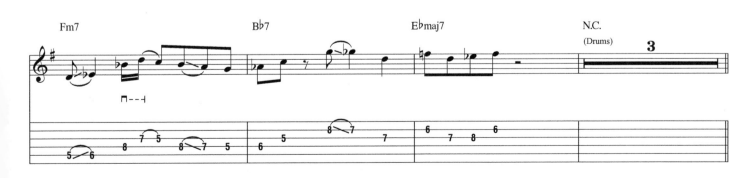

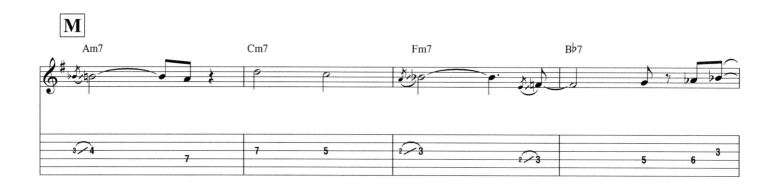

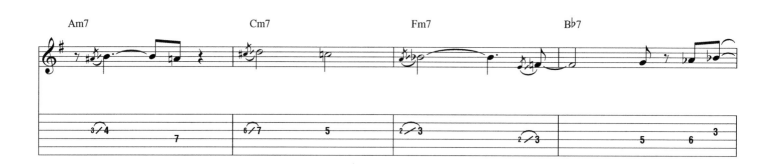

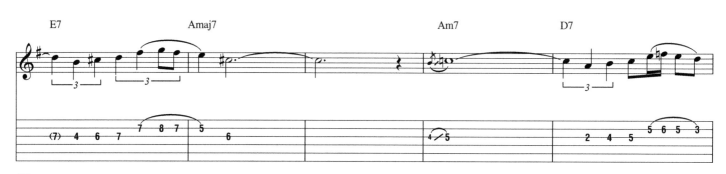

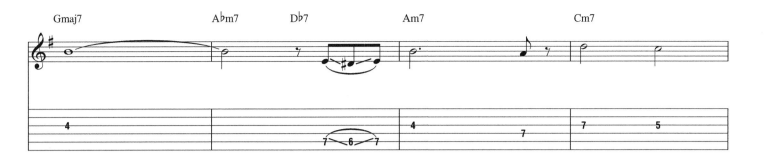

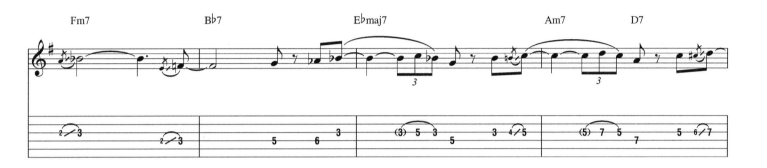

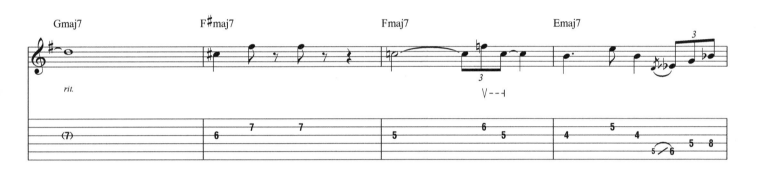

Free time

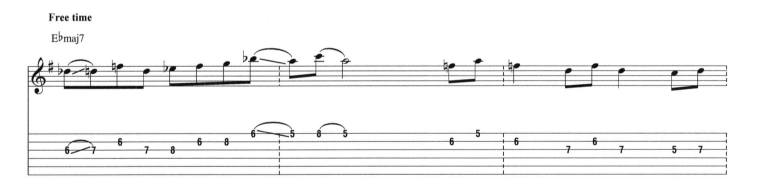

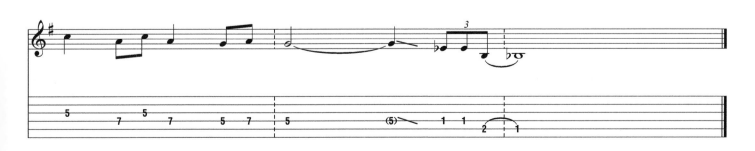

from *Joyous Lake*
Line Games
By Pat Martino

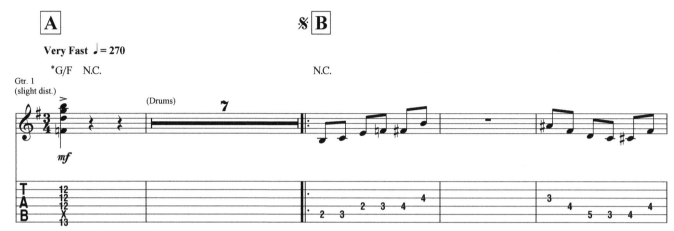

*Chord symbols reflect overall harmony.

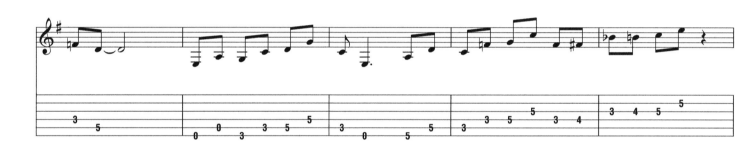

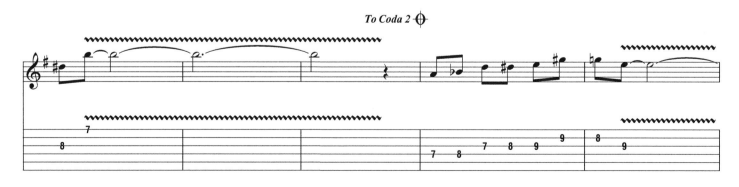

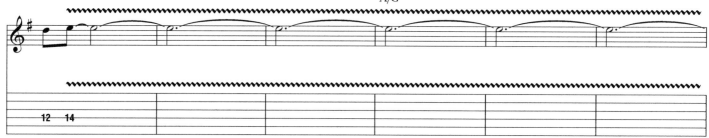

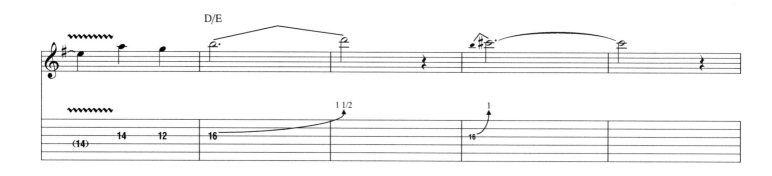

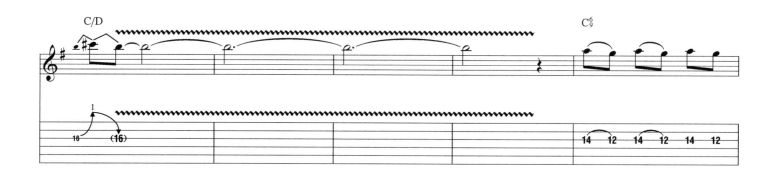

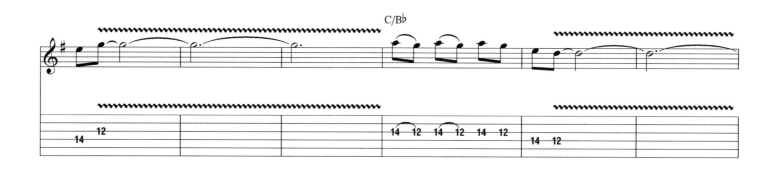

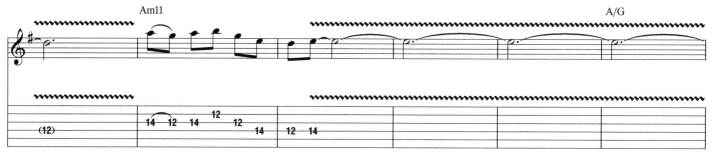

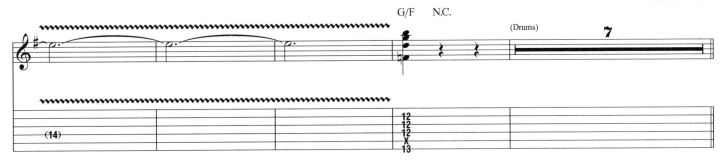

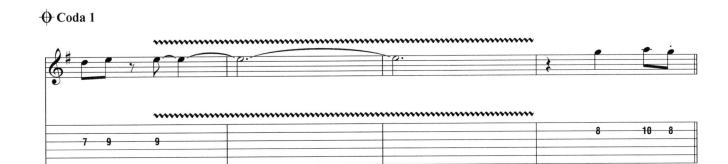

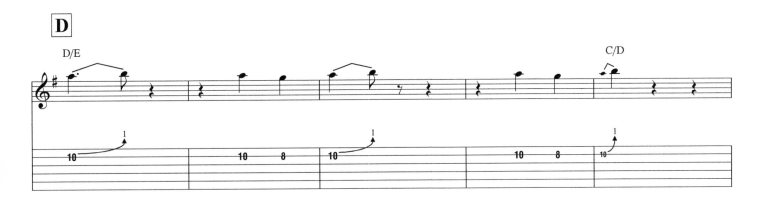

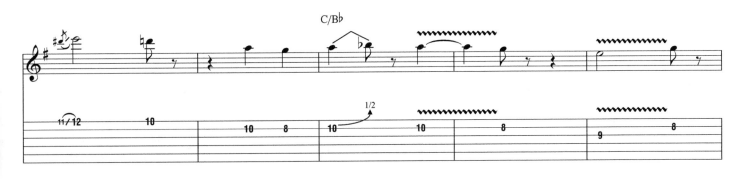

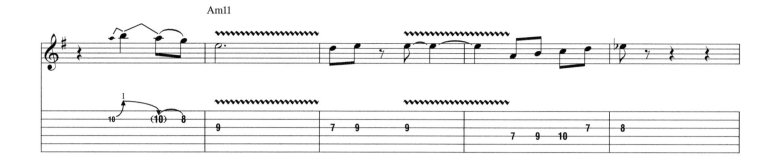

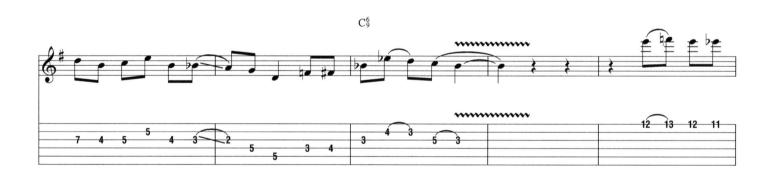

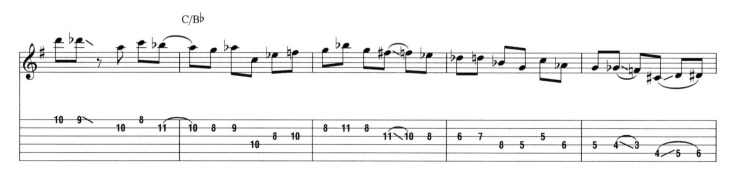

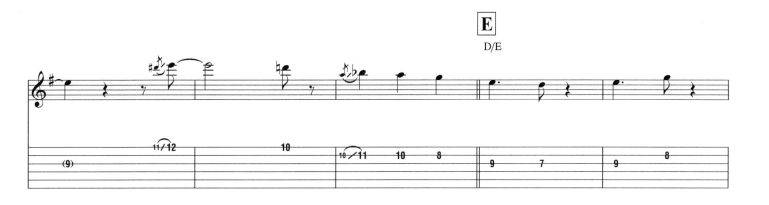

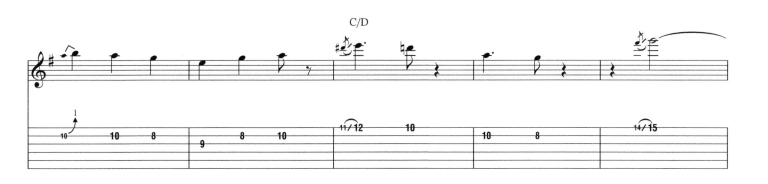

A/G

D/E

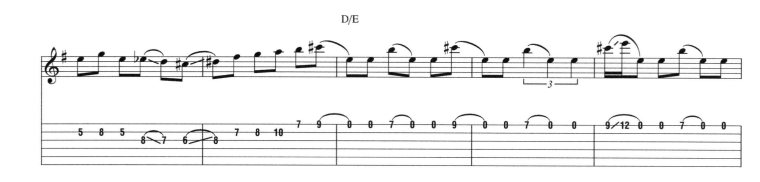

C/D

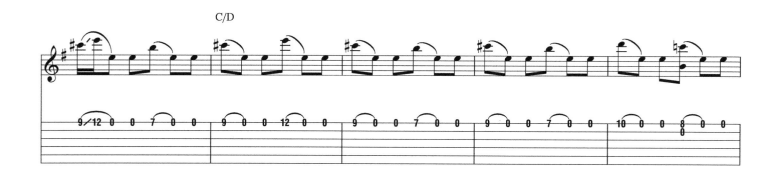

C6/9   C/B♭

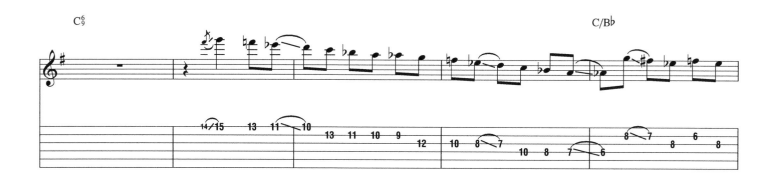

Am11

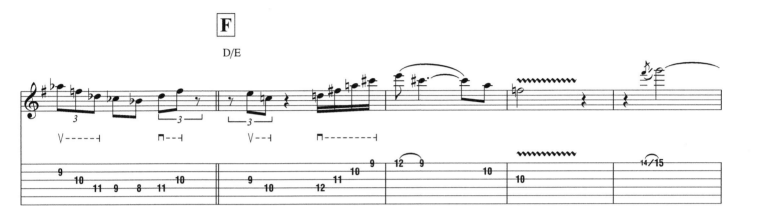

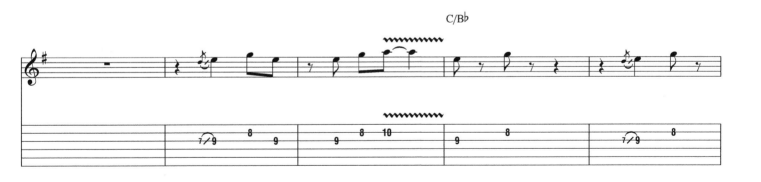

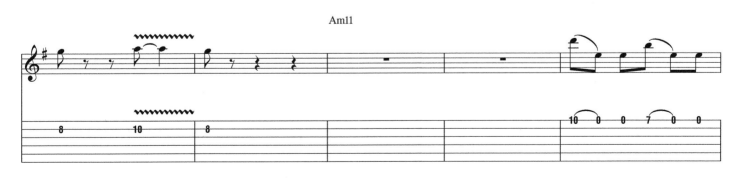

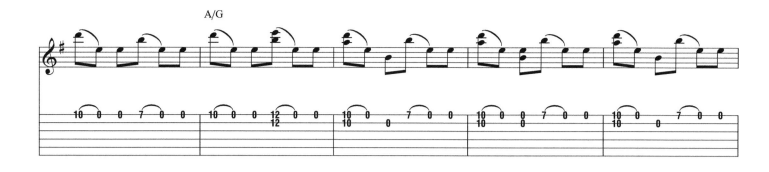

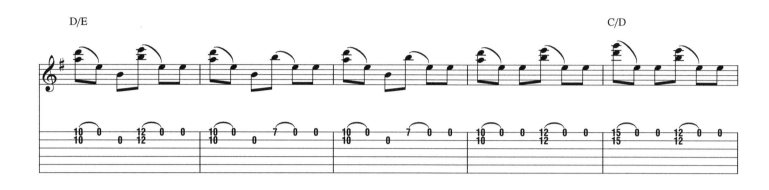

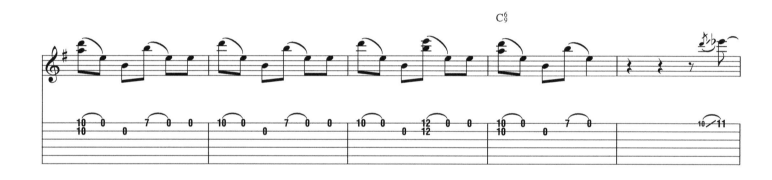

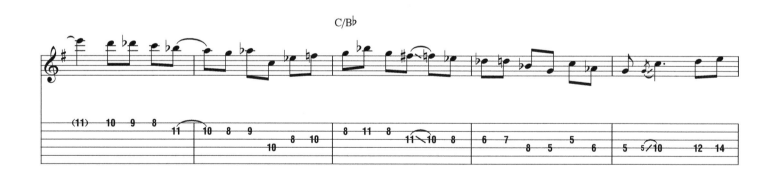

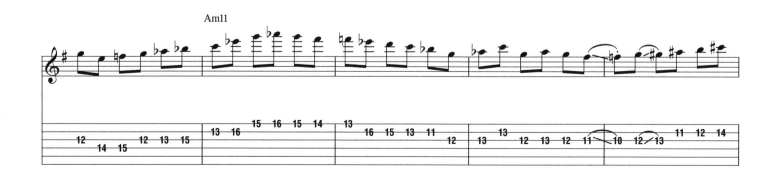

G

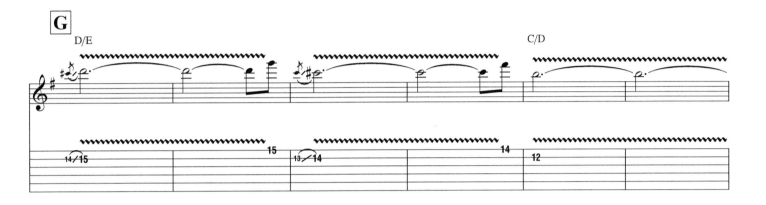

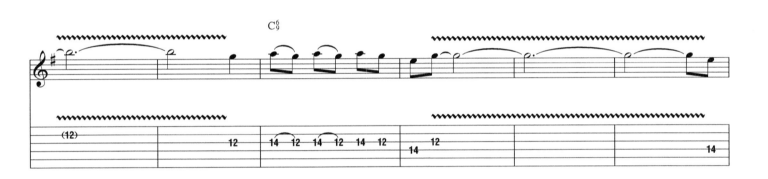

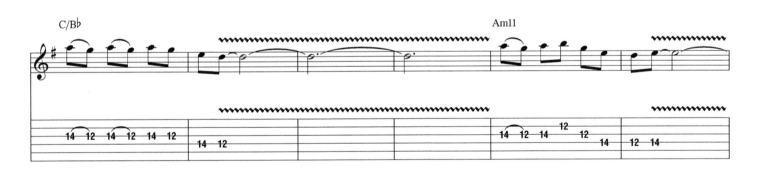

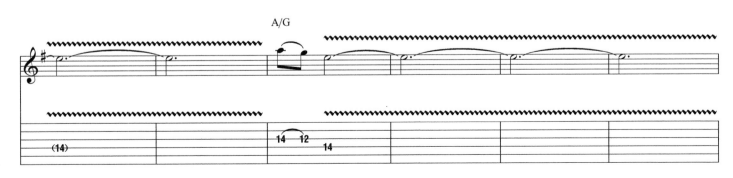

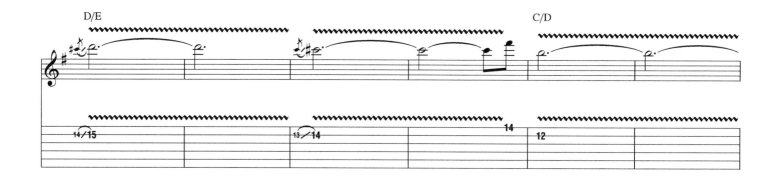

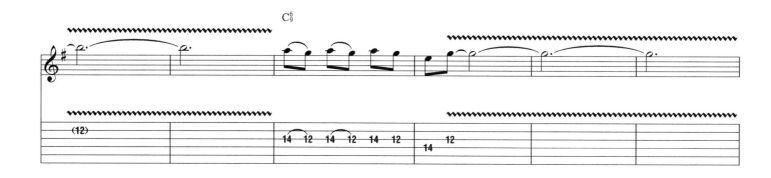

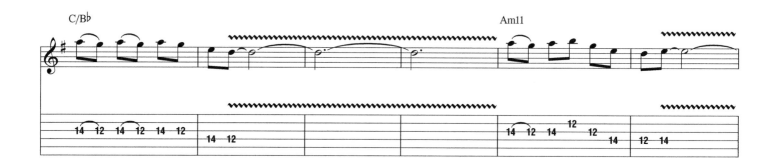

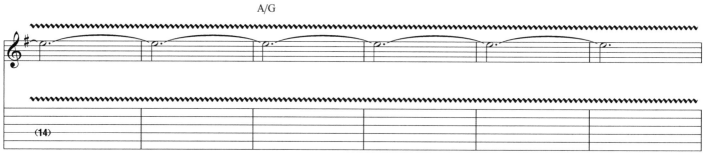

D.S. al Coda 2

Coda 2

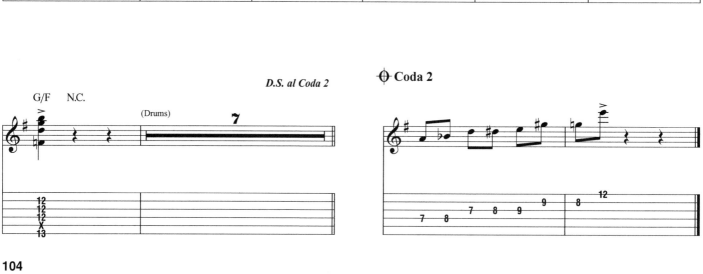

from *Desperado*
Oleo
By Sonny Rollins

*Chord symbols reflect overall harmony.

**First four courses of strings strung and tuned unison; fifth and sixth strings left individual (10 strings total).

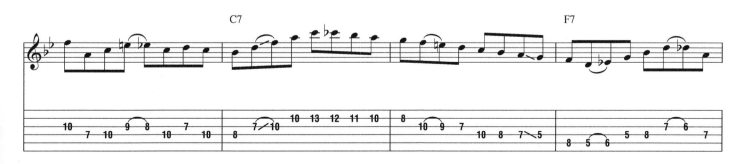

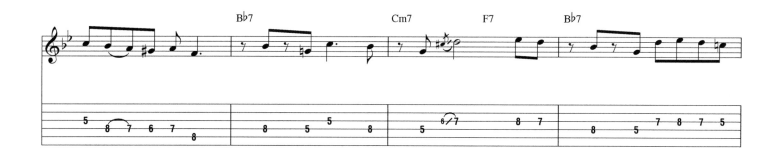

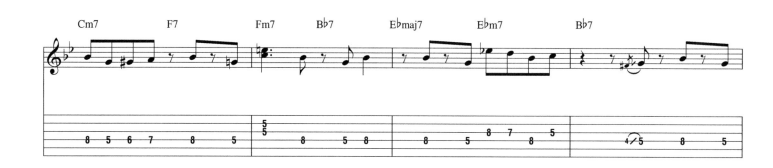

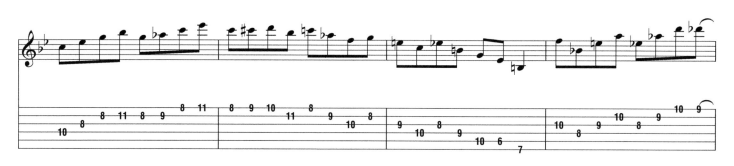

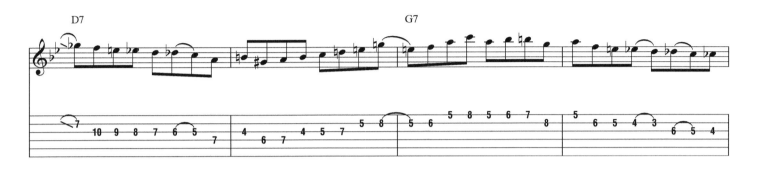

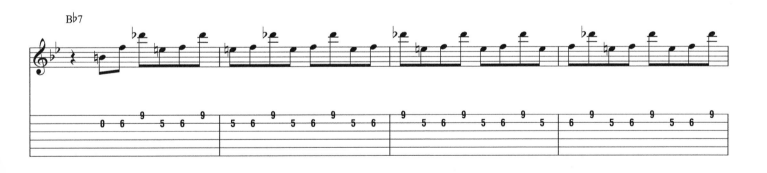

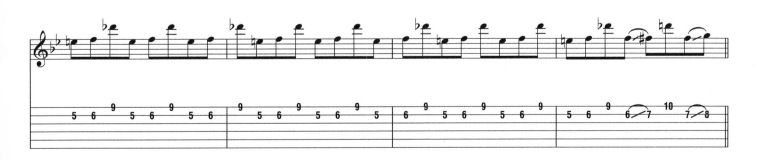

107

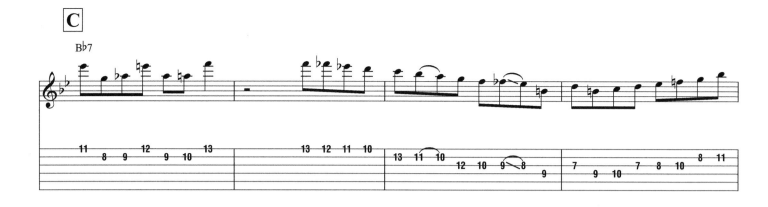

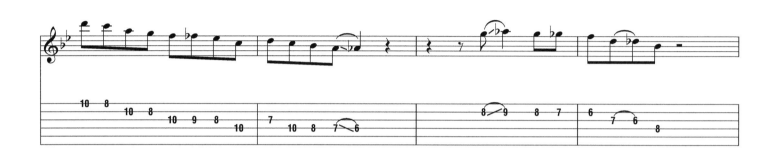

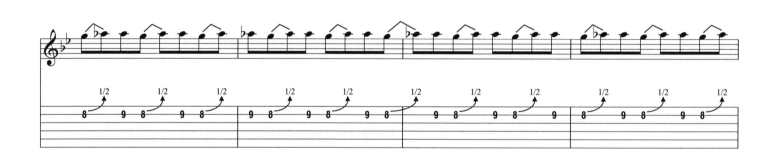

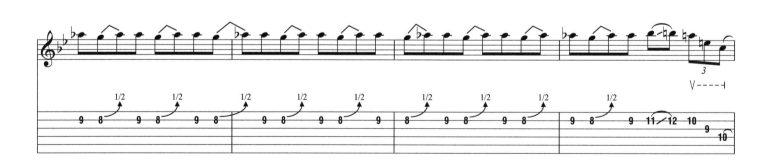

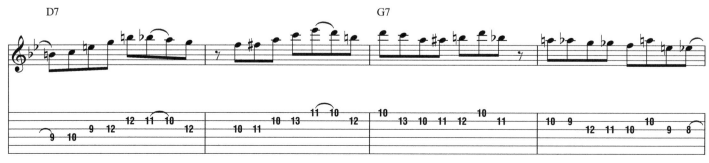

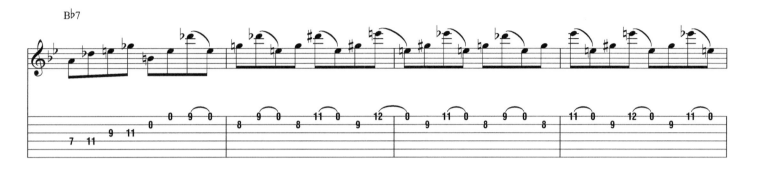

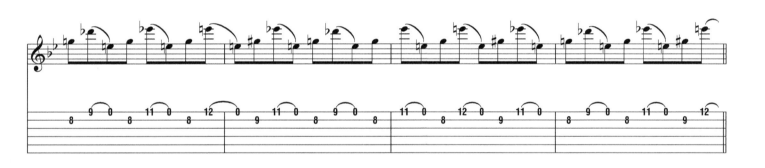

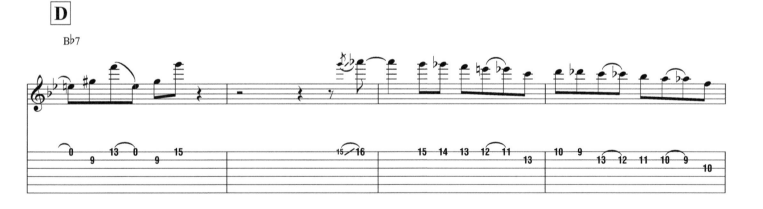

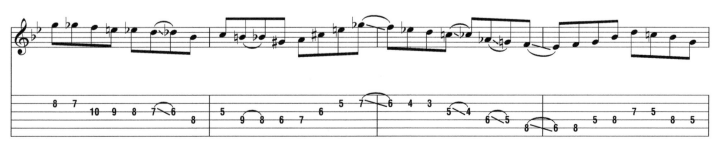

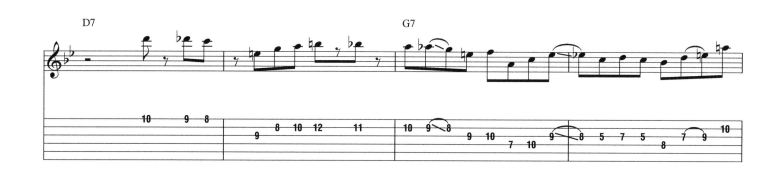

E

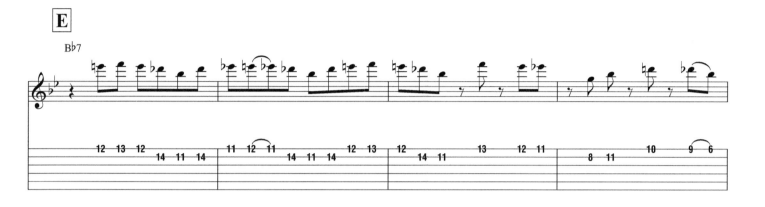

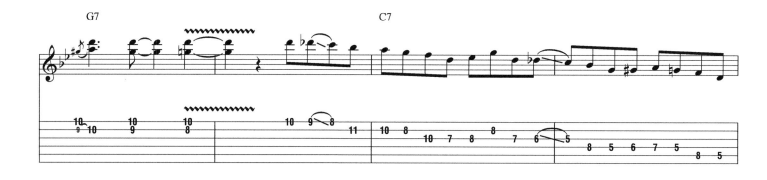

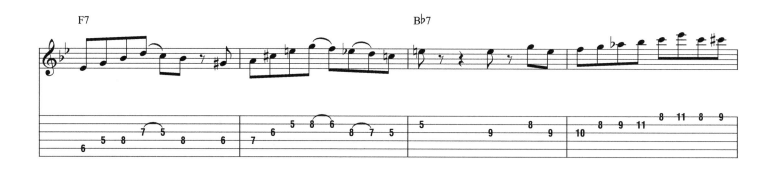

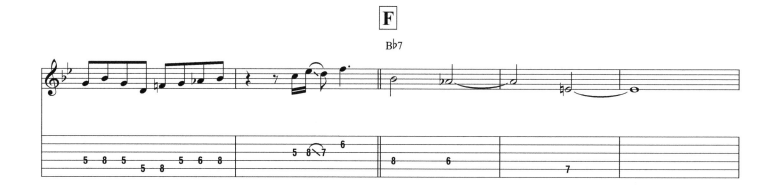

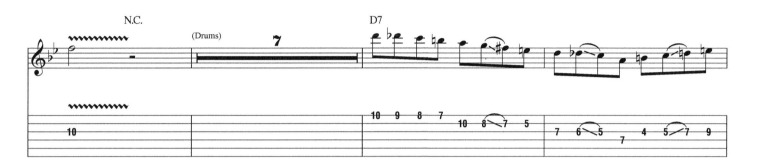

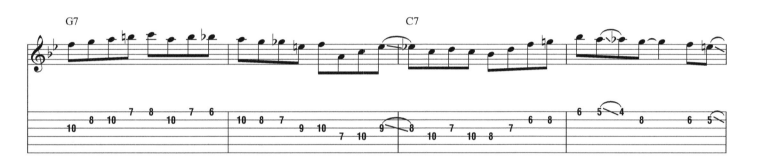

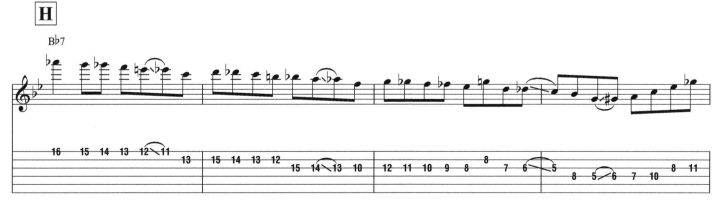

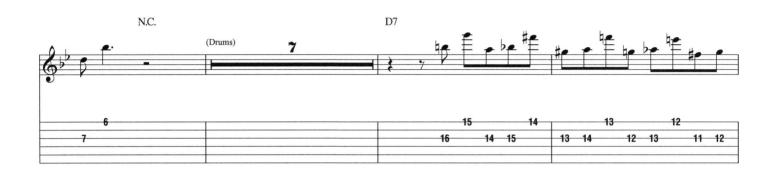

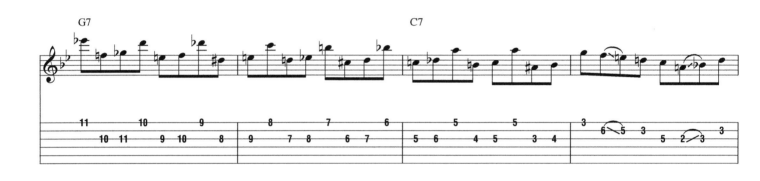

I

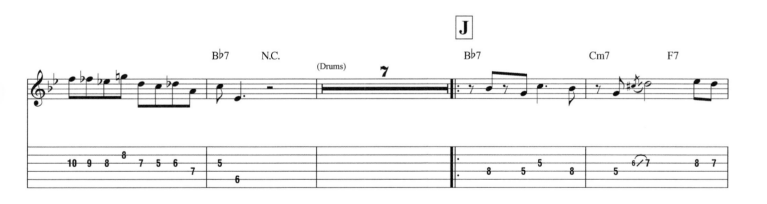

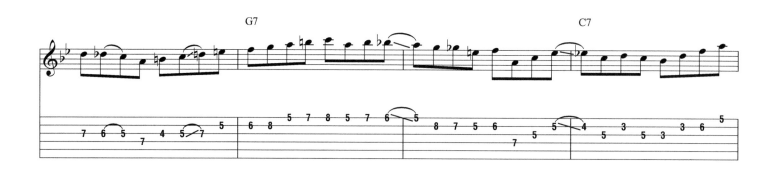

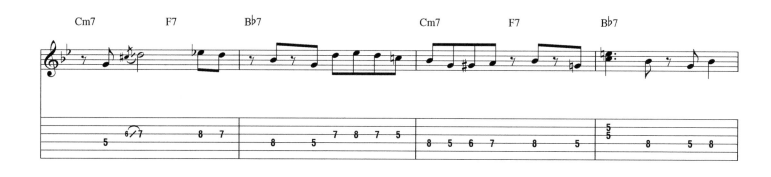

from *El Hombre*

Once I Loved
(Amor Em Paz)
(Love in Peace)

Music by Antonio Carlos Jobim
Portuguese Lyrics by Vinicius de Moraes
English Lyrics by Ray Gilbert

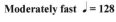

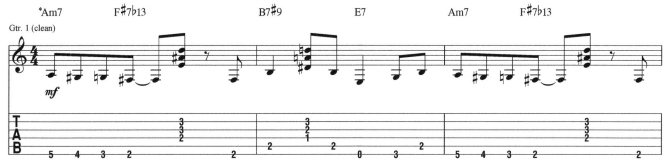

*Chord symbols reflect overall harmony.

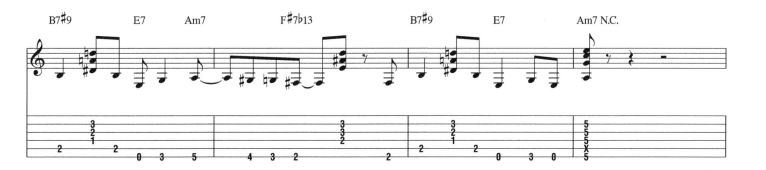

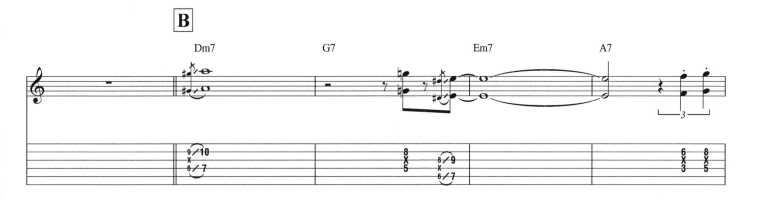

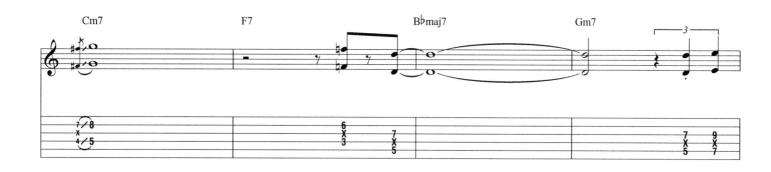

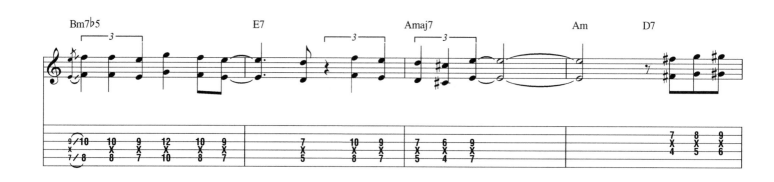

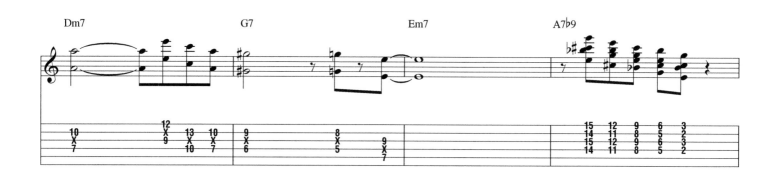

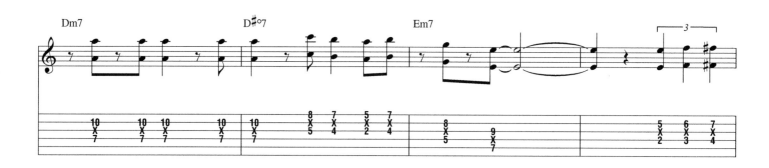

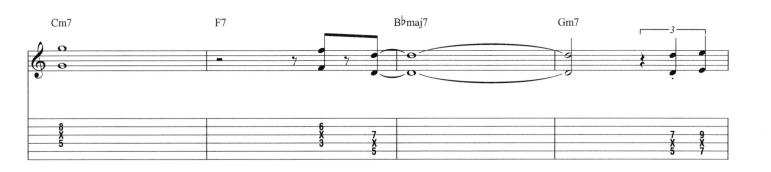

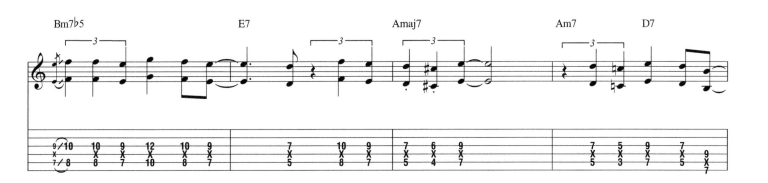

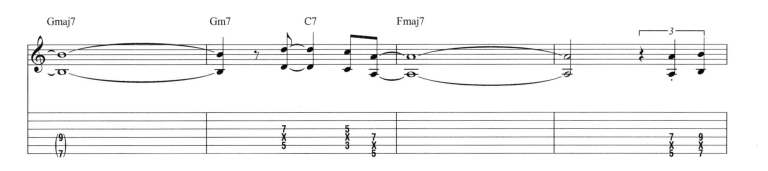

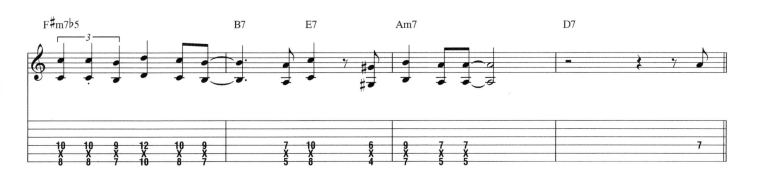

C

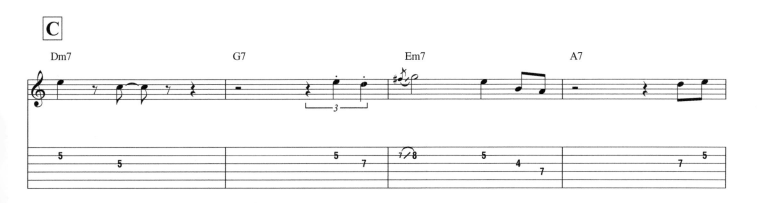

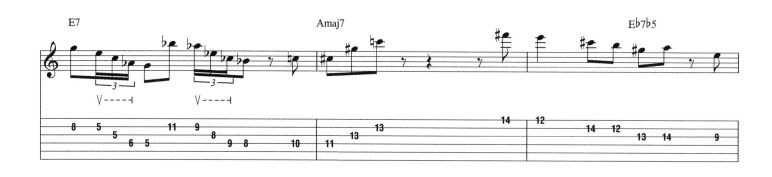

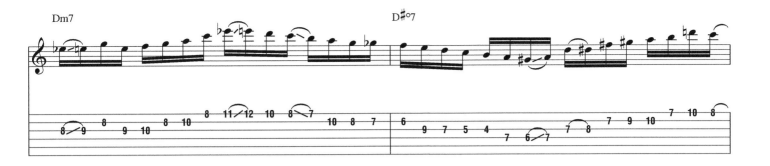

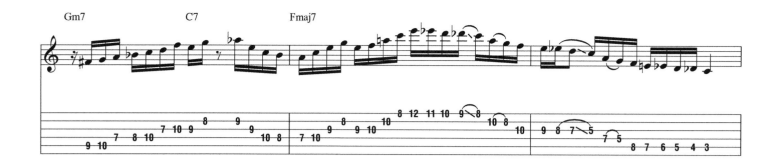

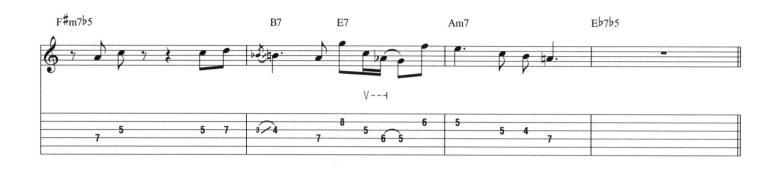

D

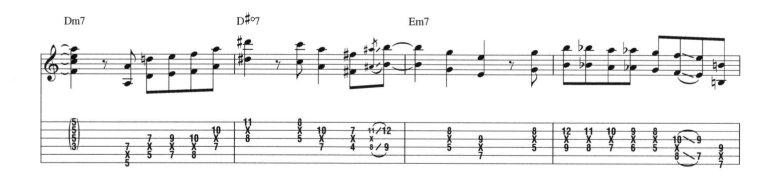

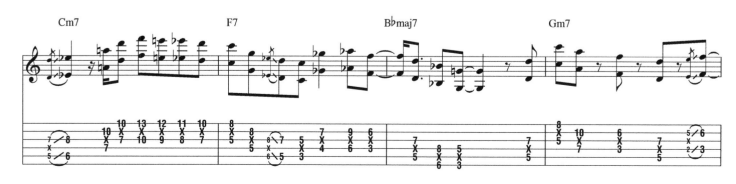

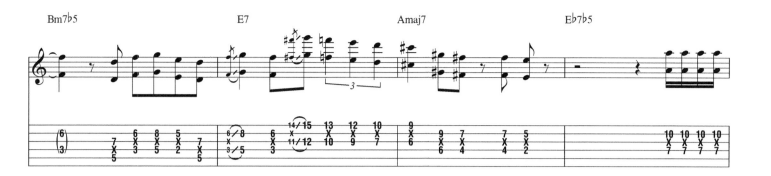

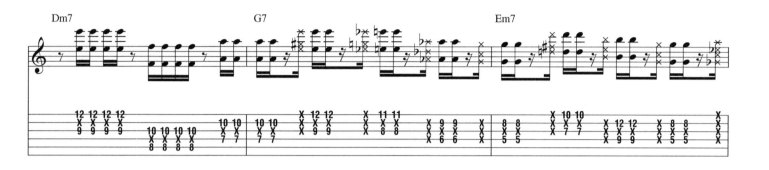

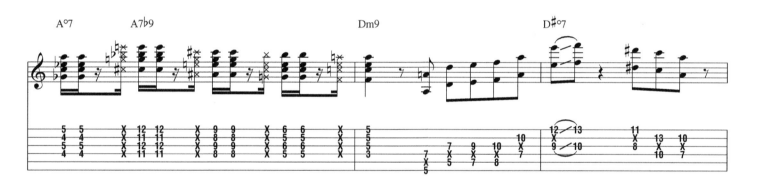

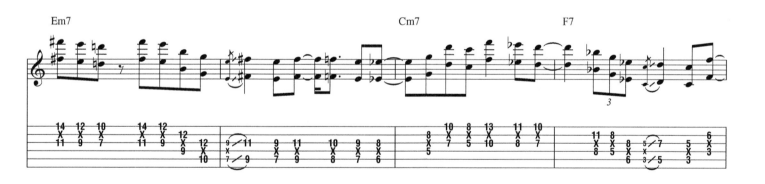

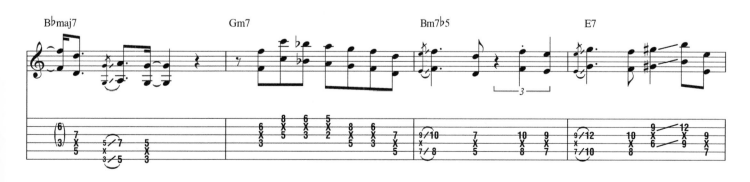

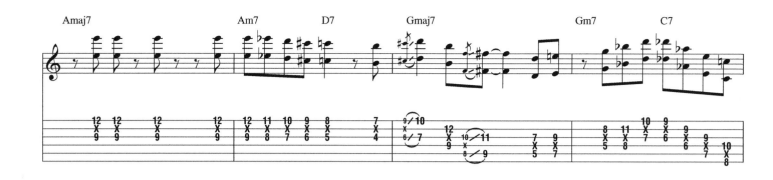

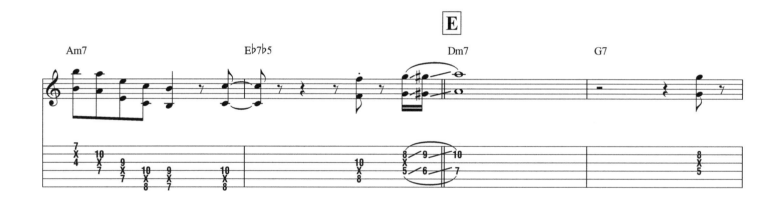

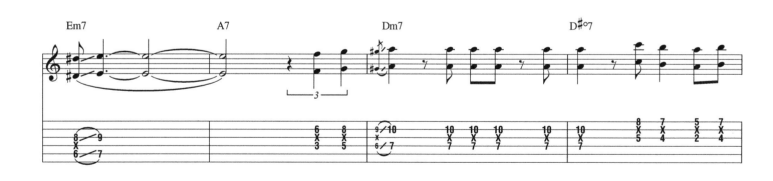

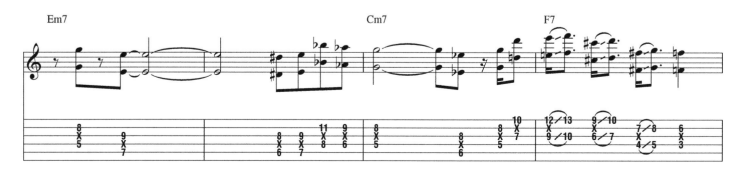

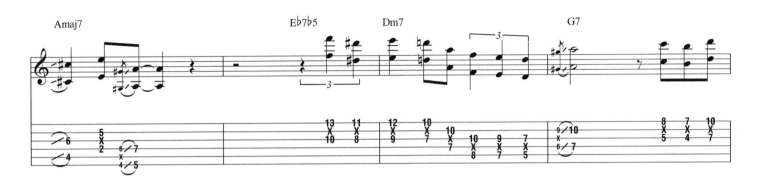

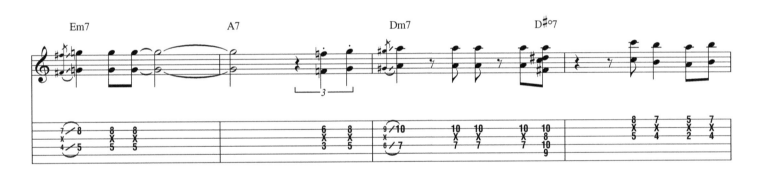

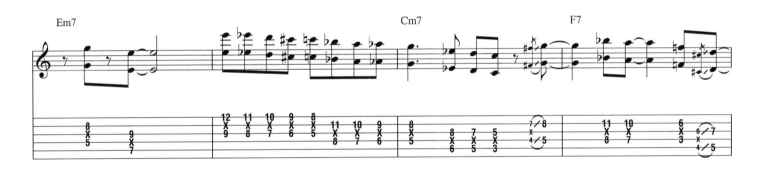

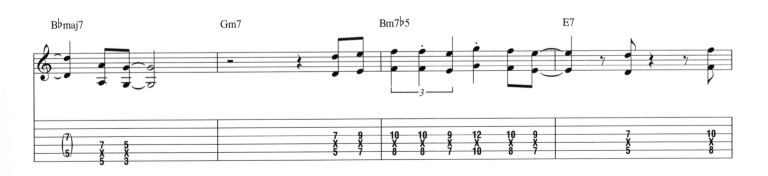

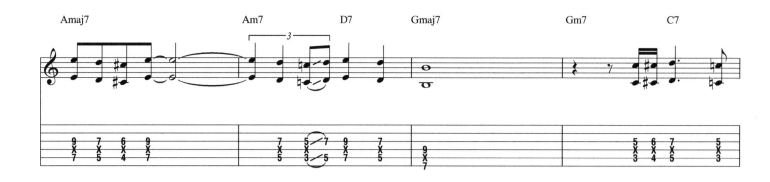

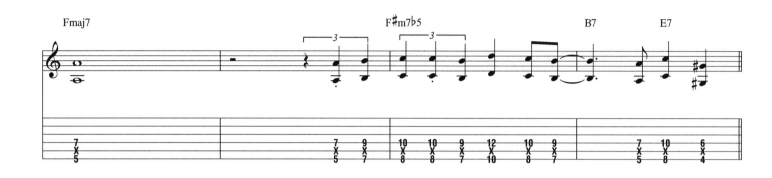

F

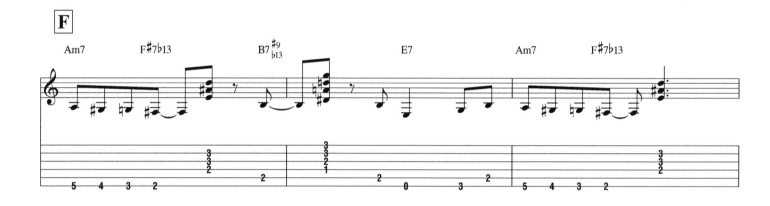

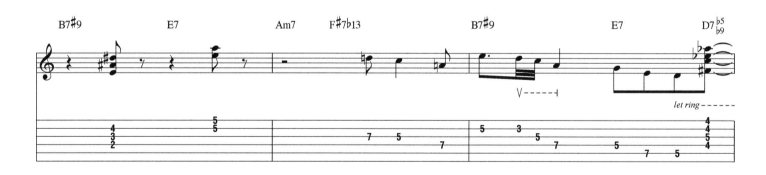

Free time

from *Live*

Sunny

Words and Music by Bobby Hebb

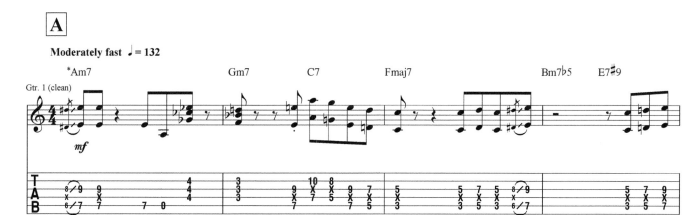

*Chord symbols reflect overall harmony.

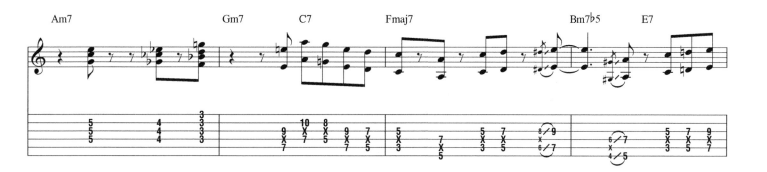

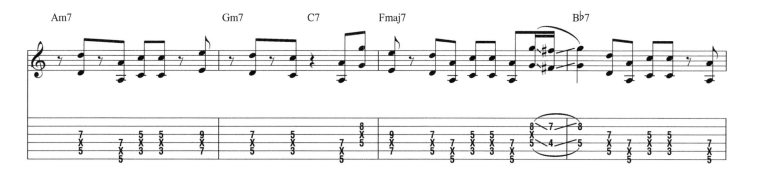

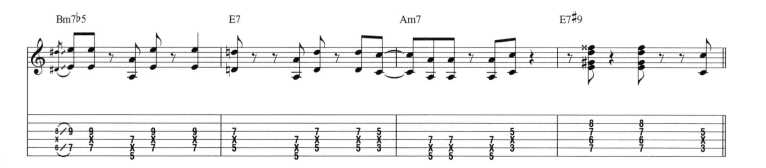

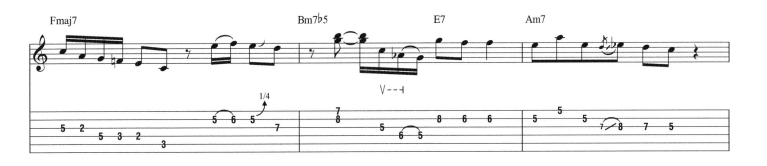

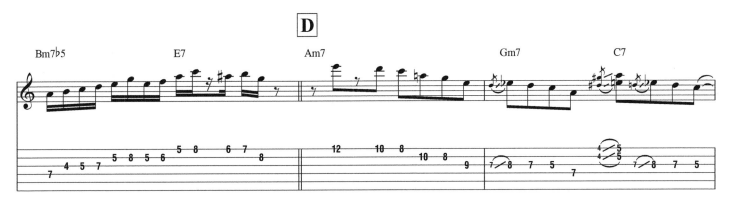

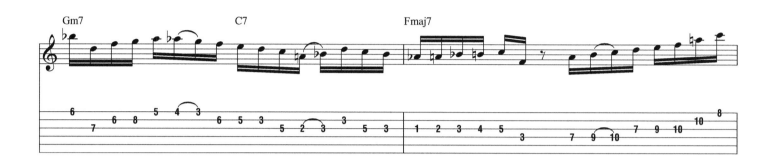

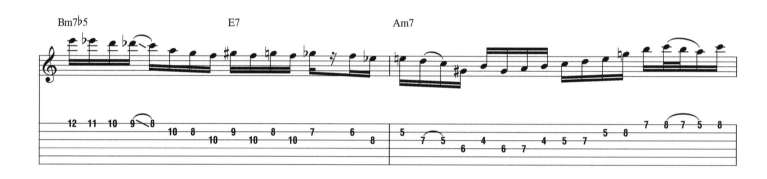

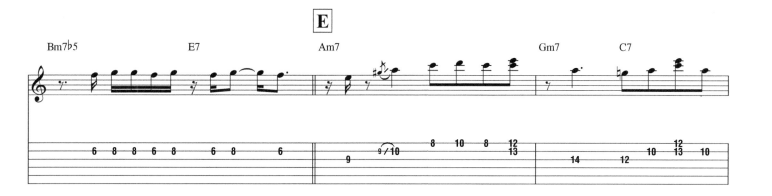

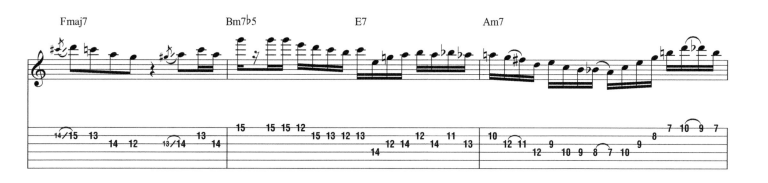

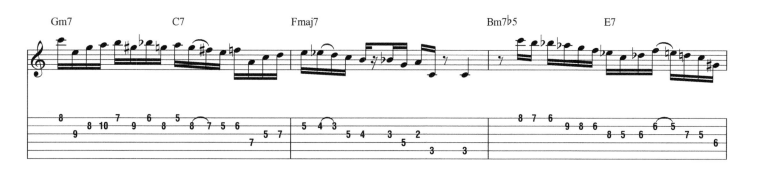

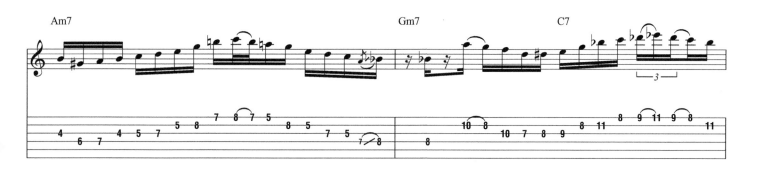

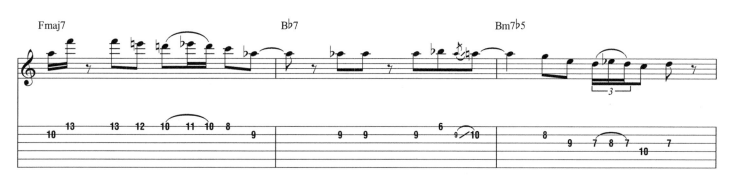

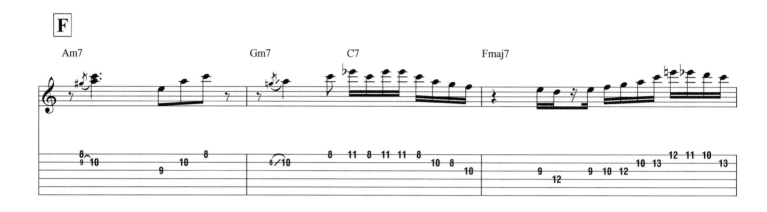

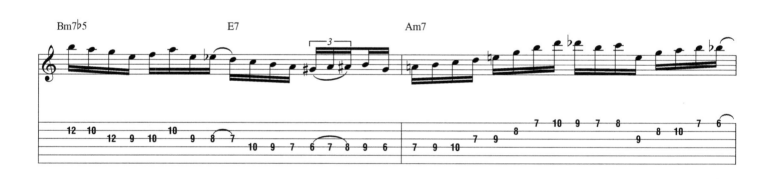

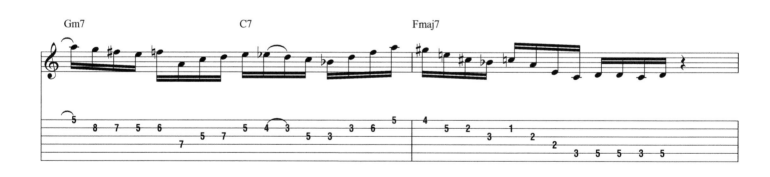

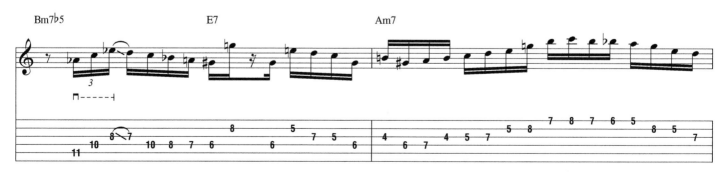

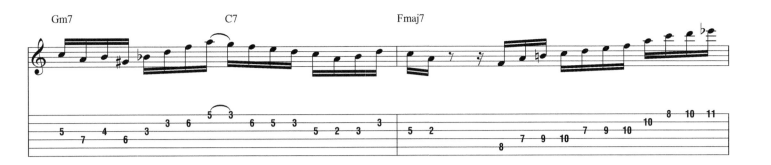

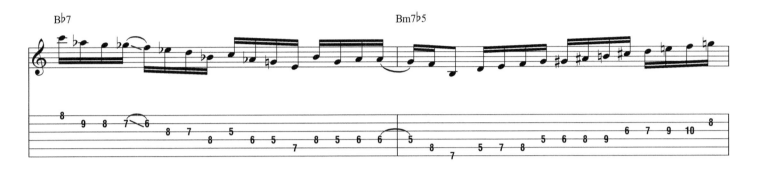

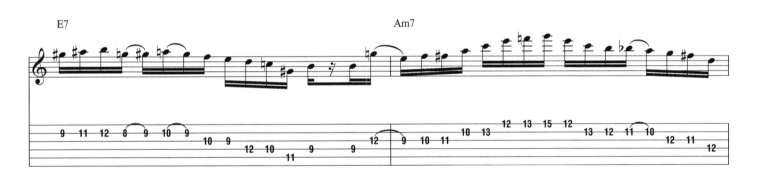

G

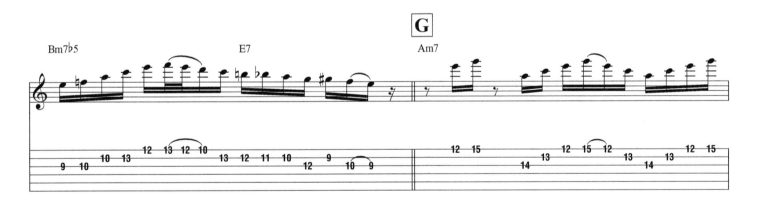

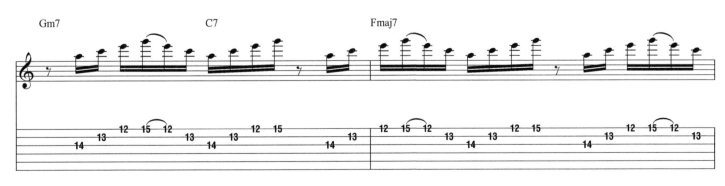

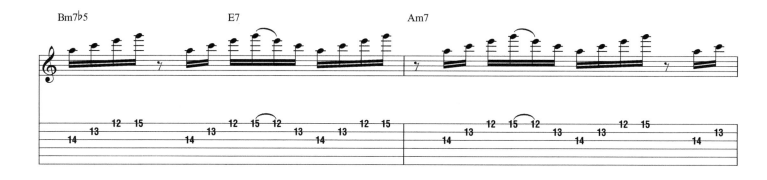

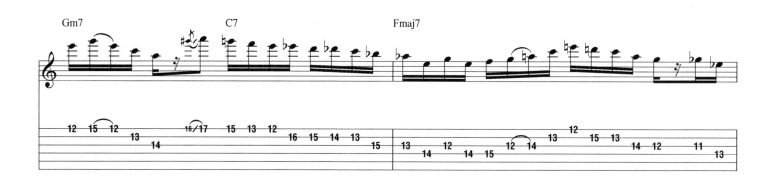

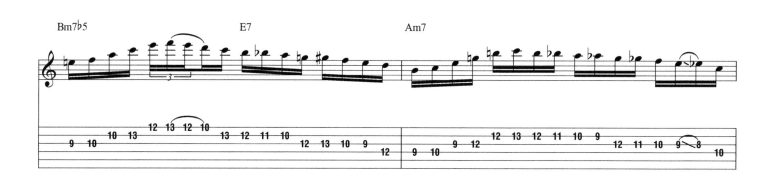

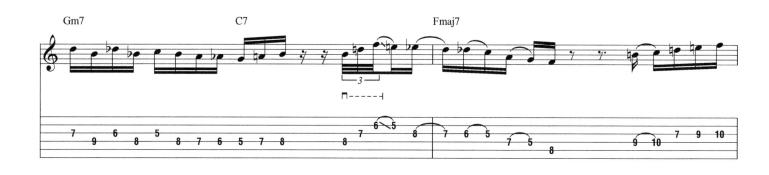

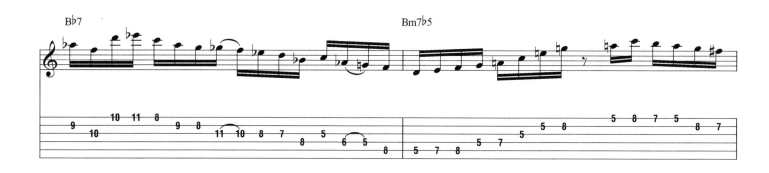

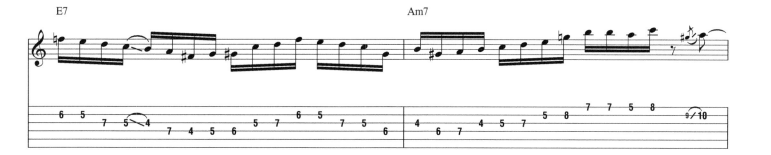

H

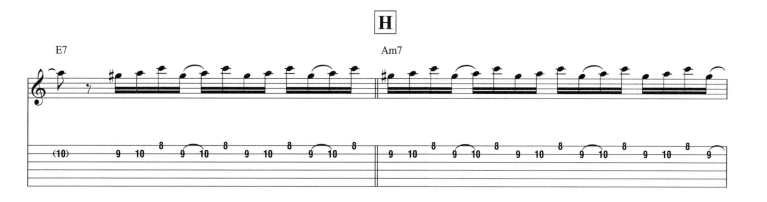

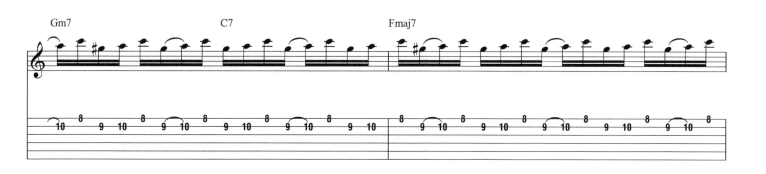

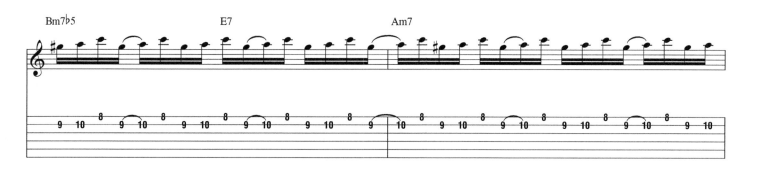

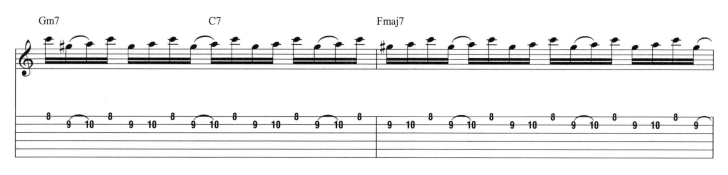

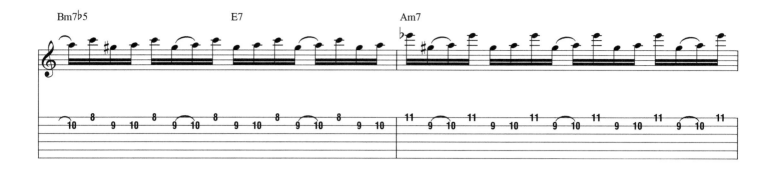

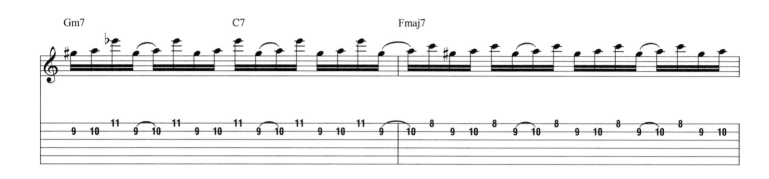

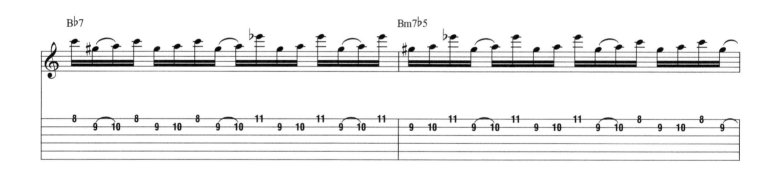

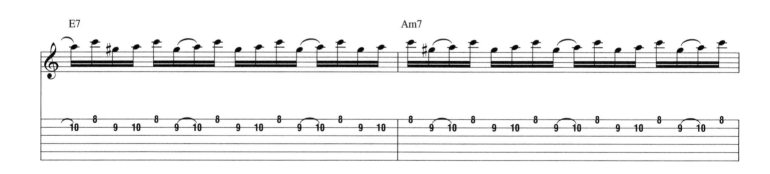

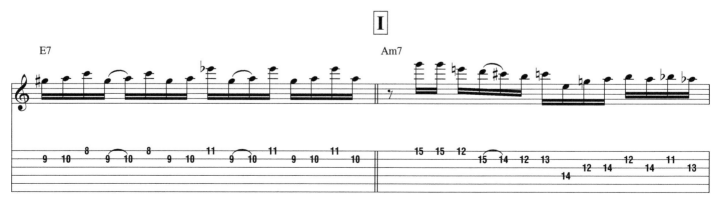

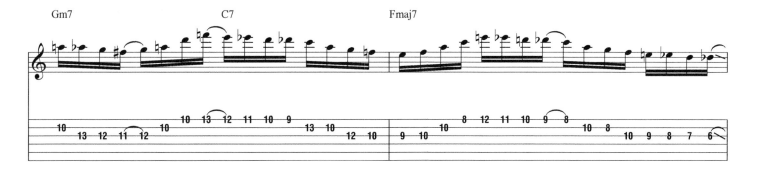

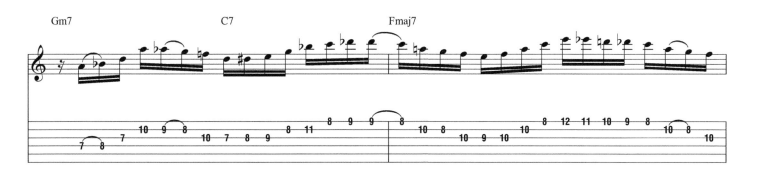

J

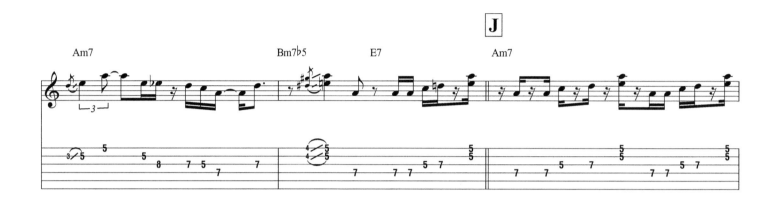

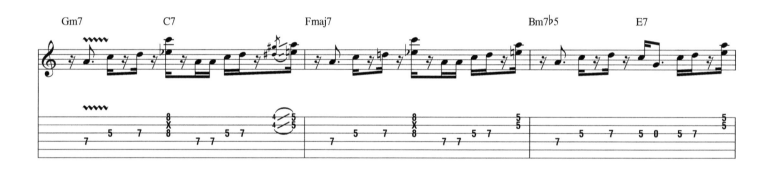

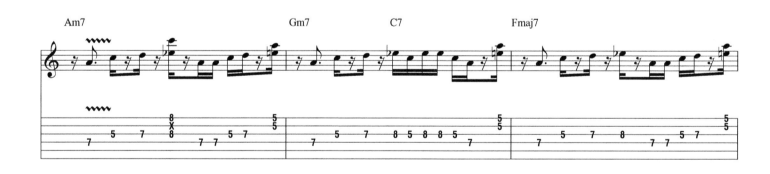

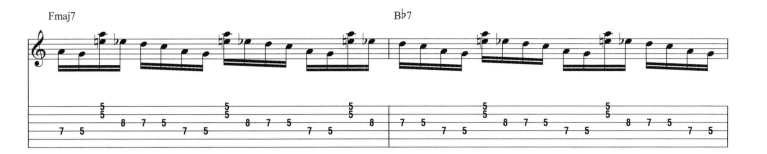

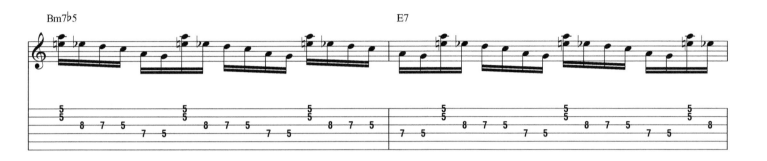

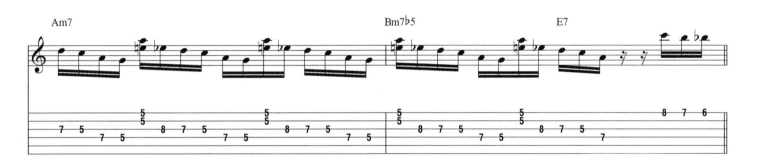

K

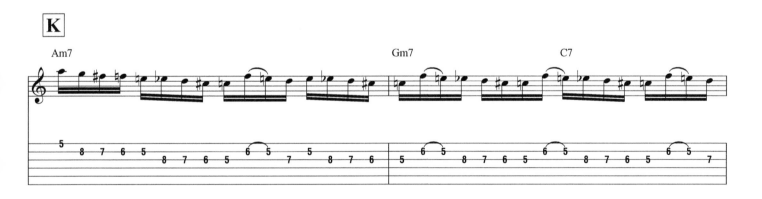

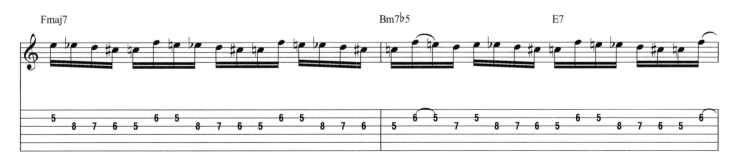

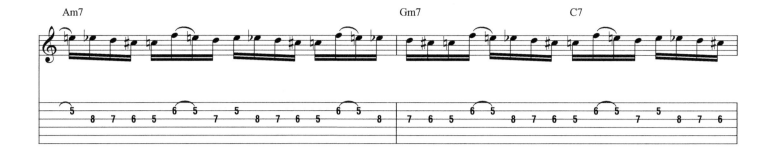

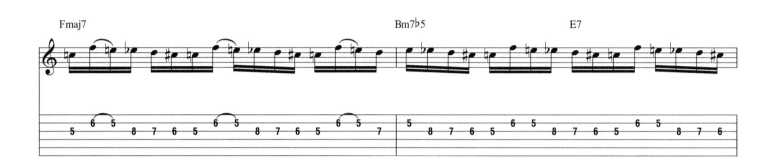

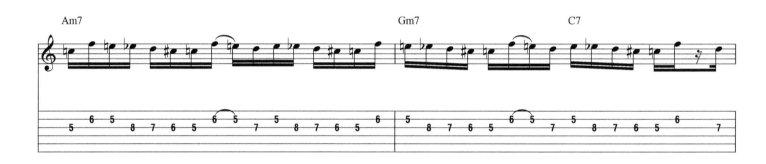

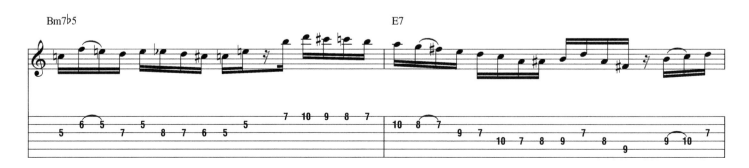

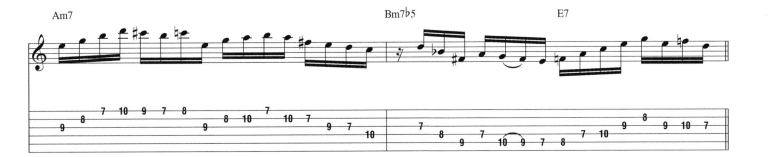

L

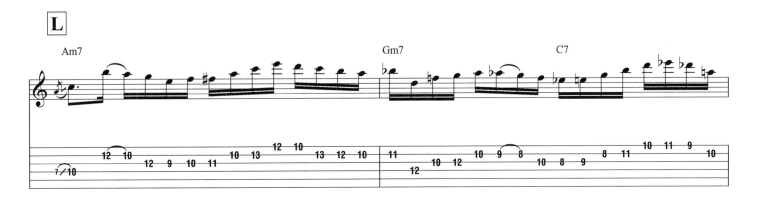

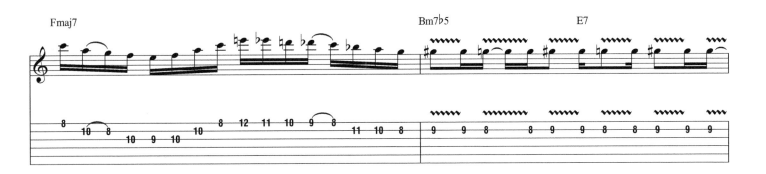

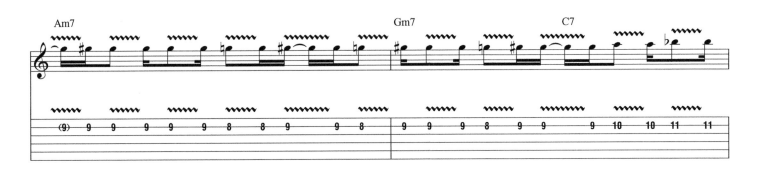

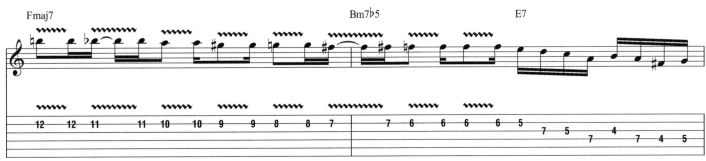

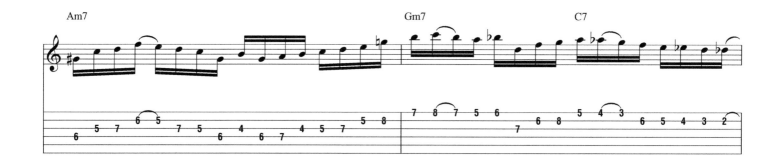

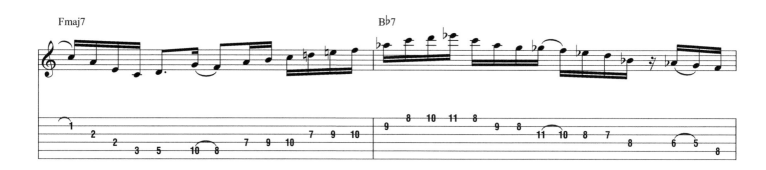

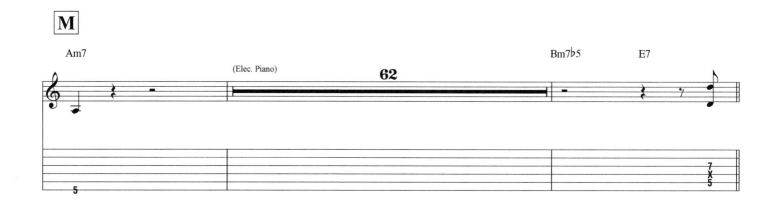

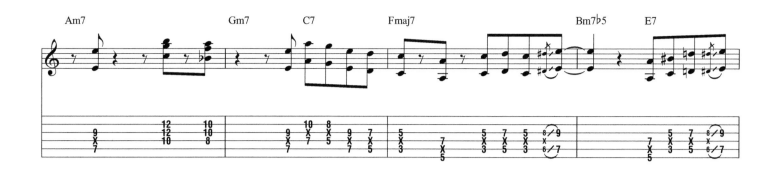

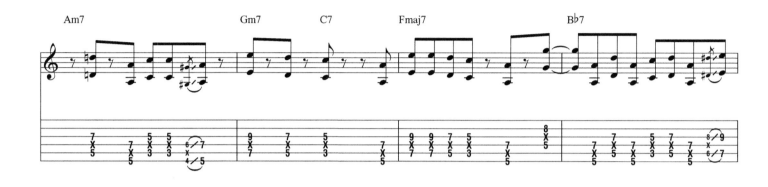

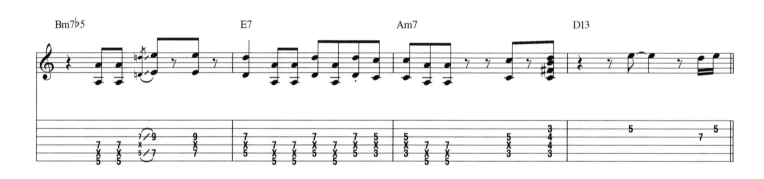

P

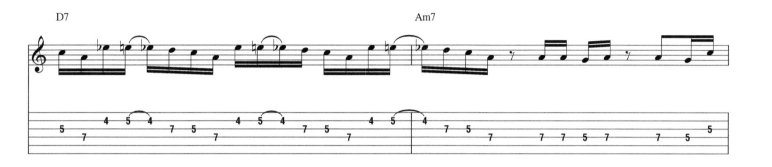

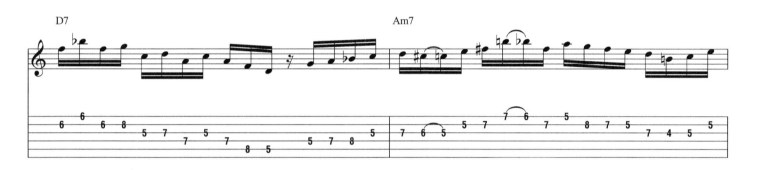

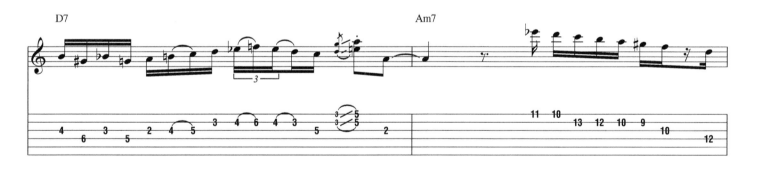

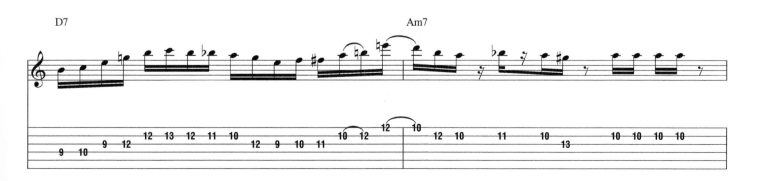

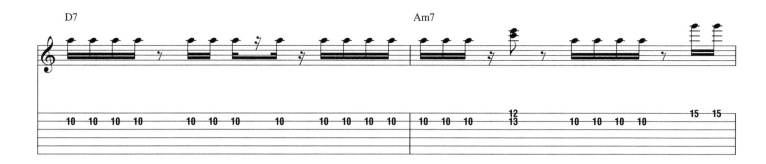

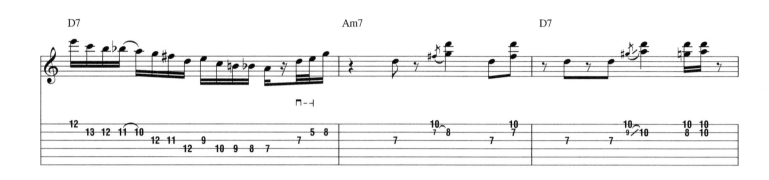

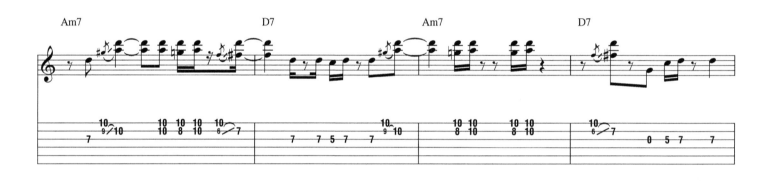

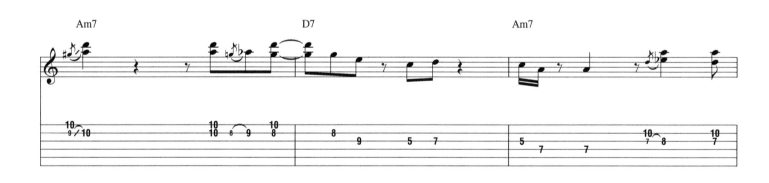

146

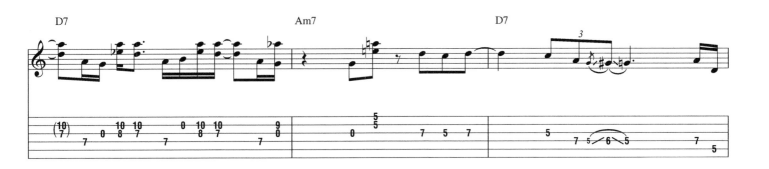

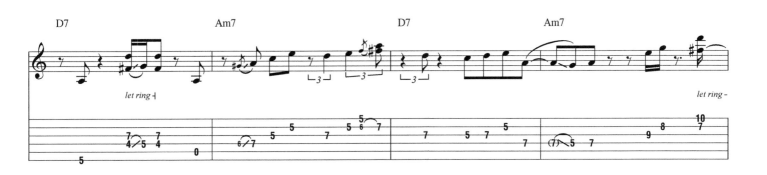

from *Comin' & Goin'*
Three Base Hit
By Pat Martino

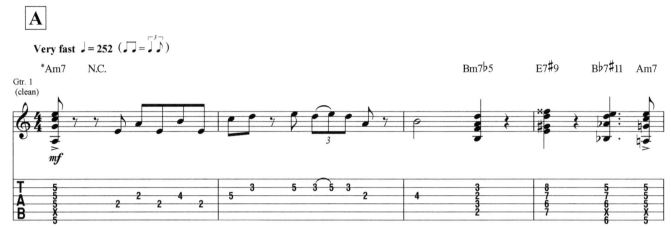

*Chord symbols reflect overall harmony.

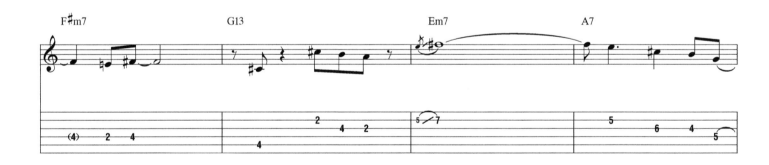

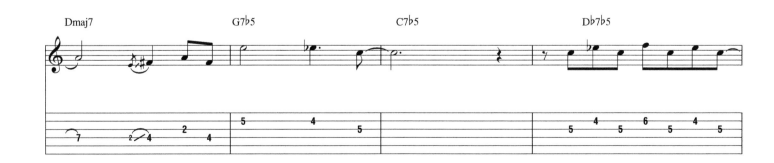

B

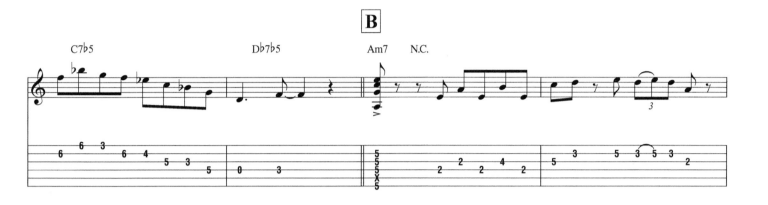

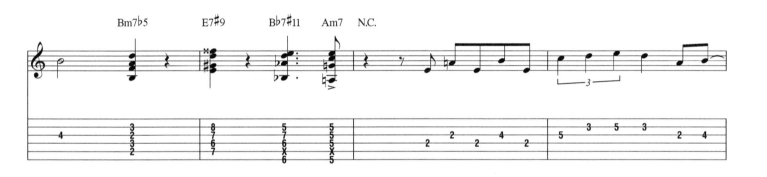

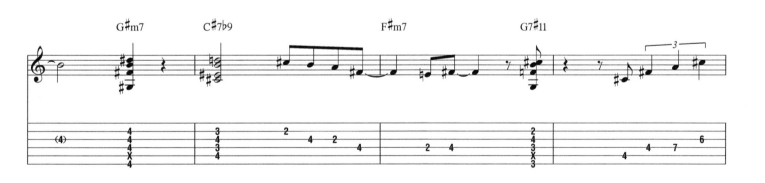

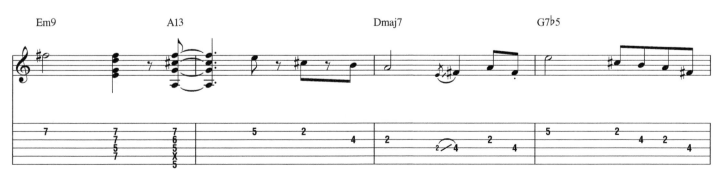

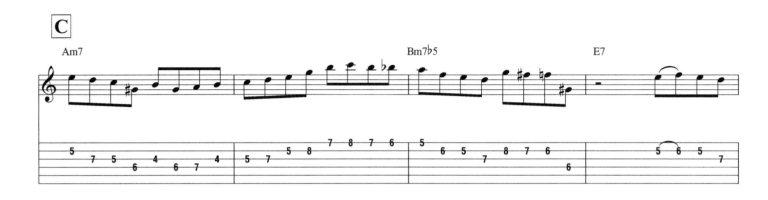

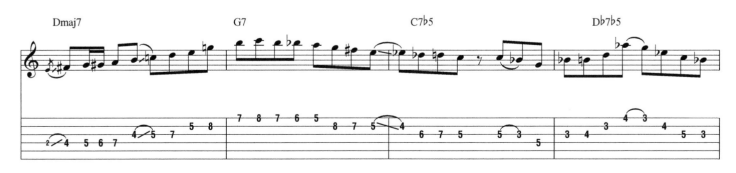

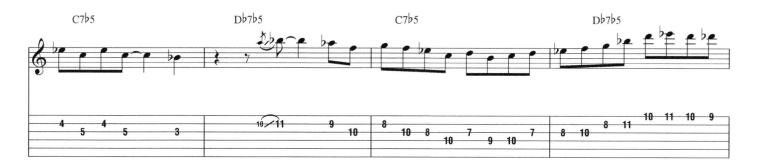

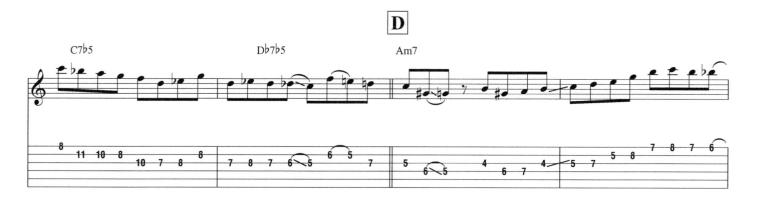

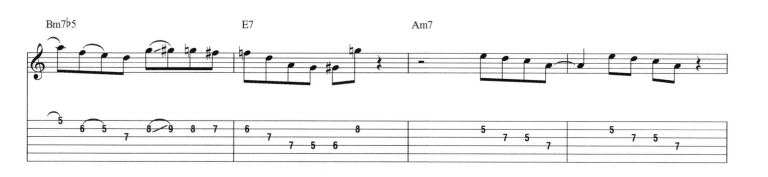

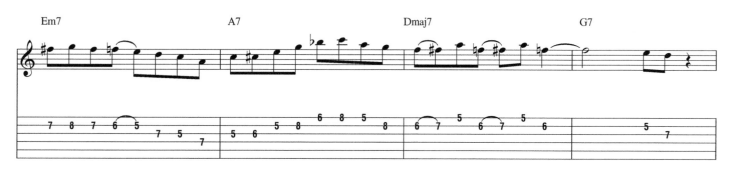

E

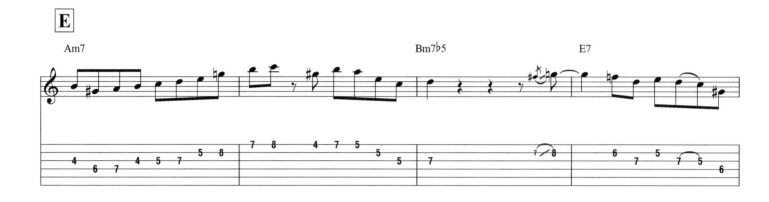

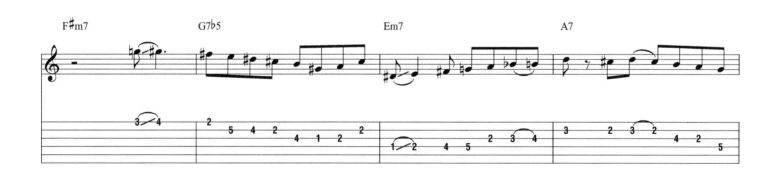

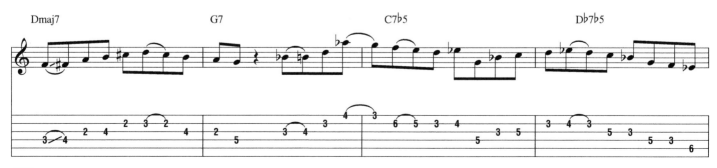

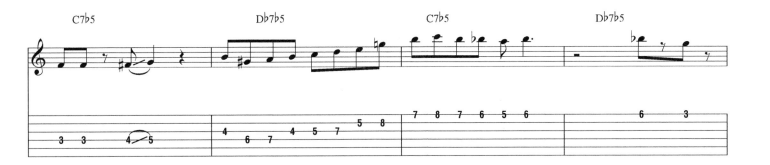

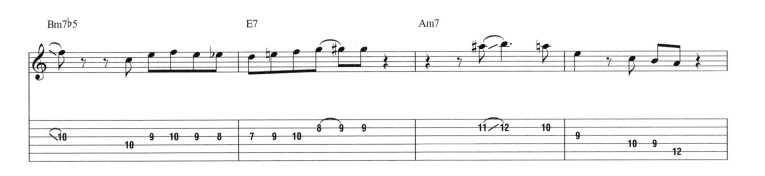

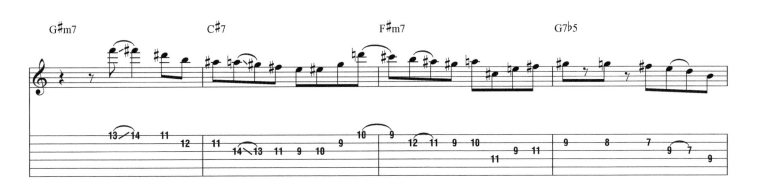

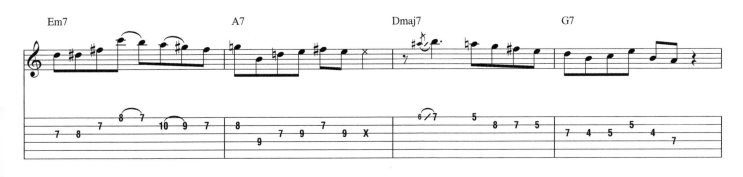

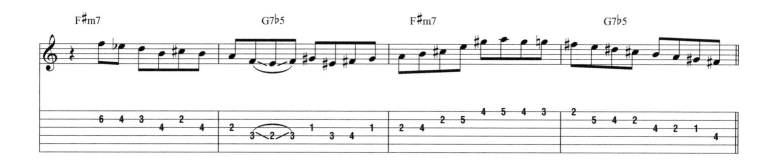

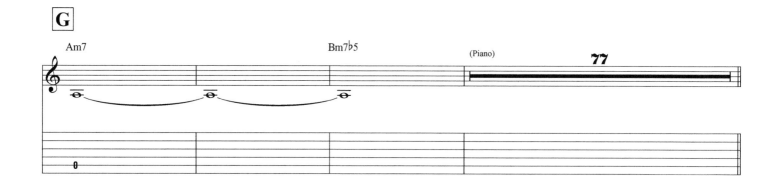

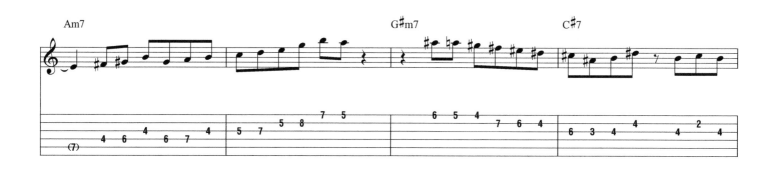

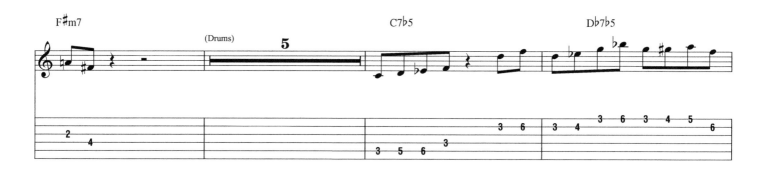

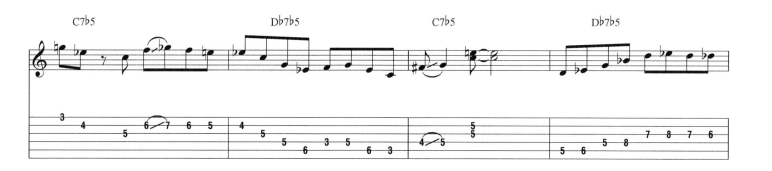

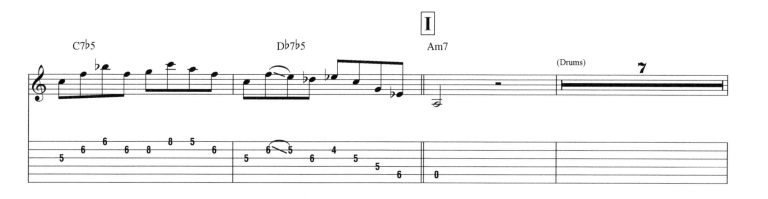

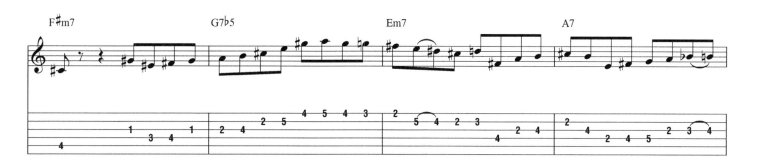

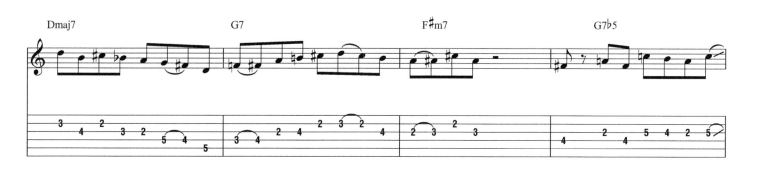

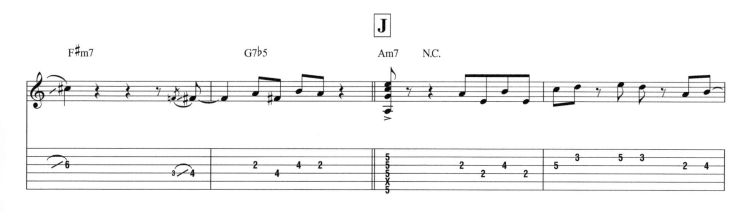

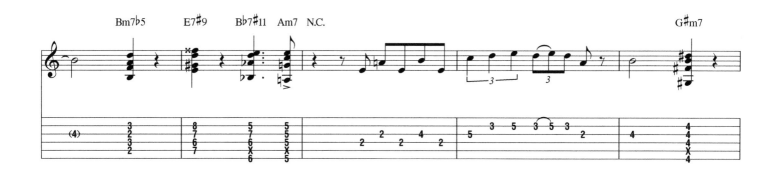

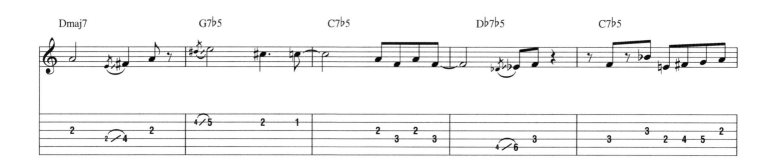

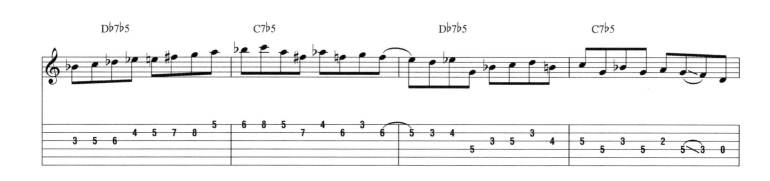

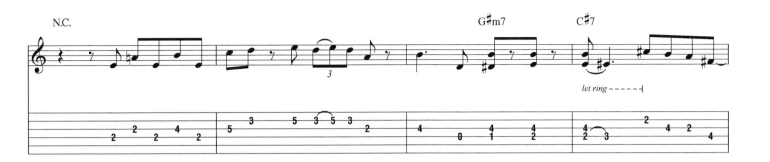

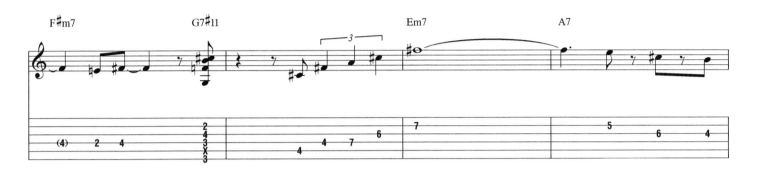

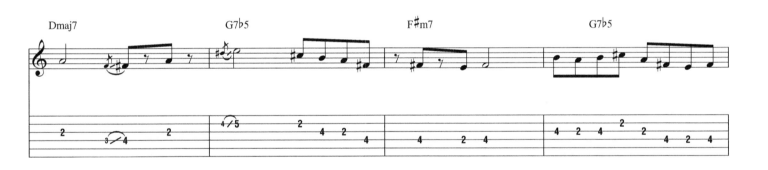

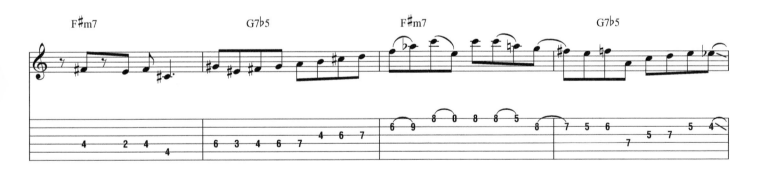

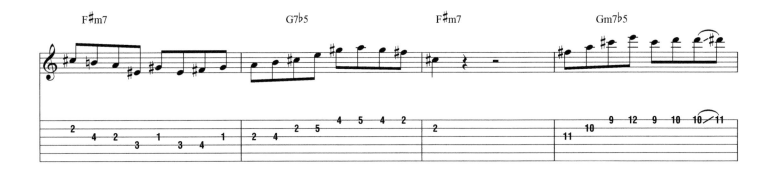

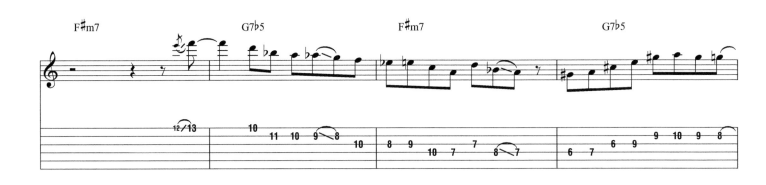

Begin fade

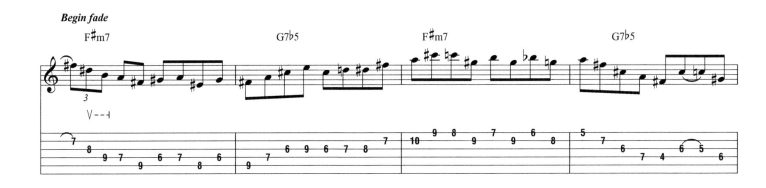

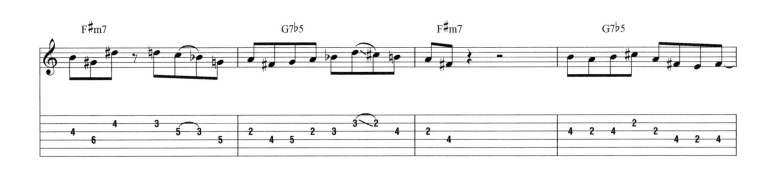

Fade out

from *East*

Trick

By Patrick Azzara

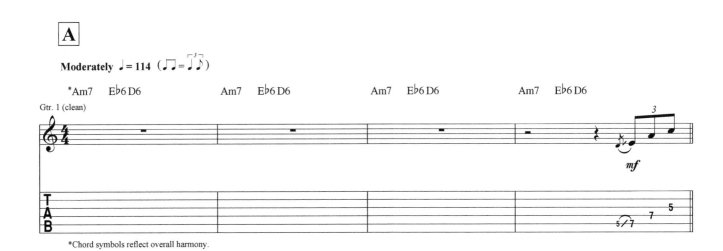

*Chord symbols reflect overall harmony.

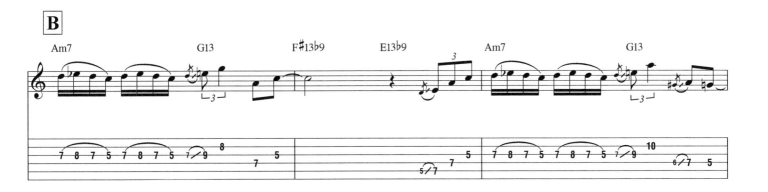

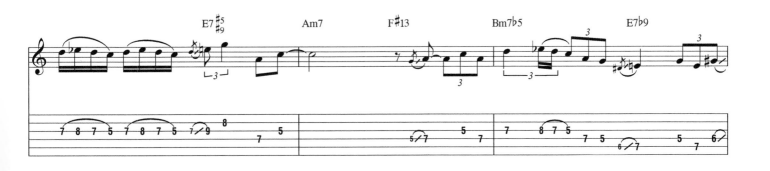

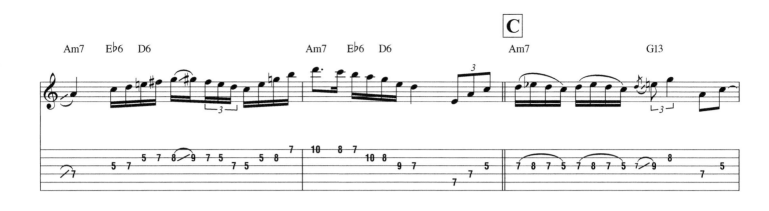

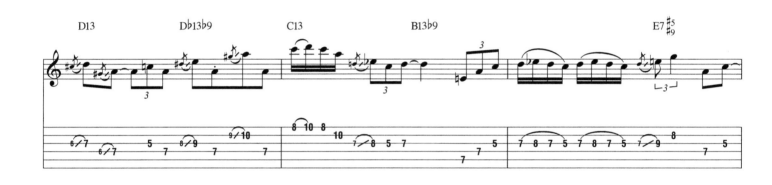

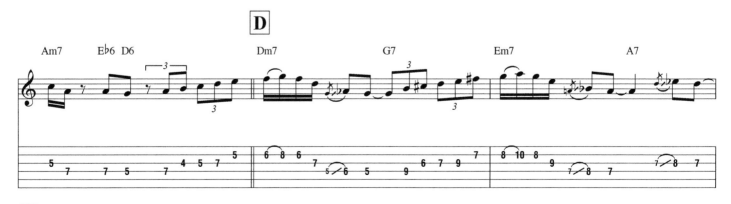

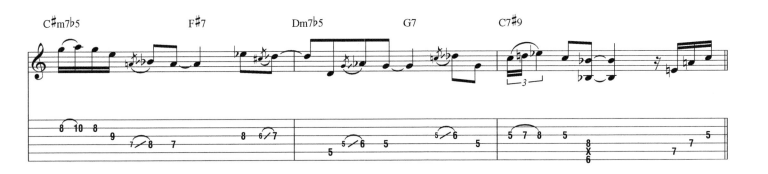

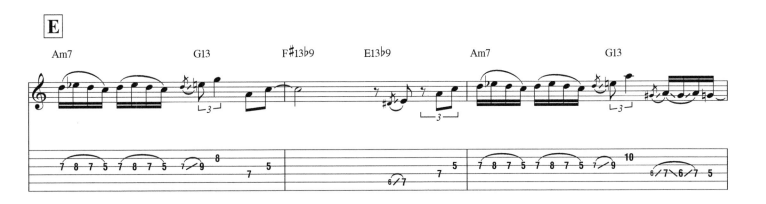

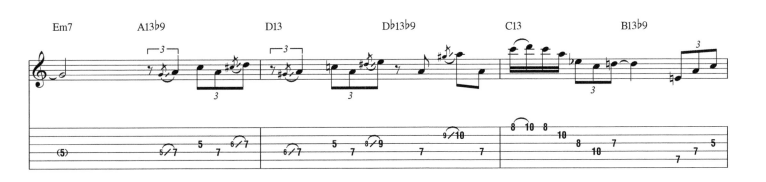

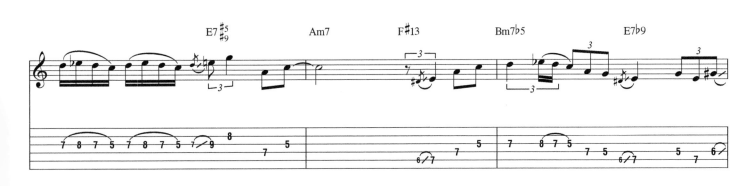

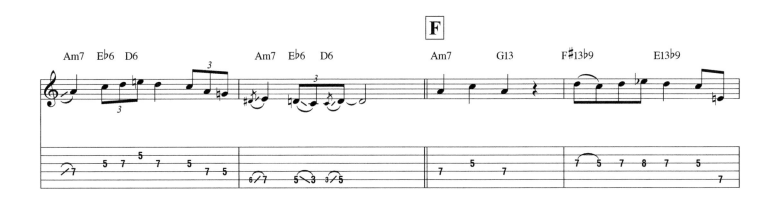

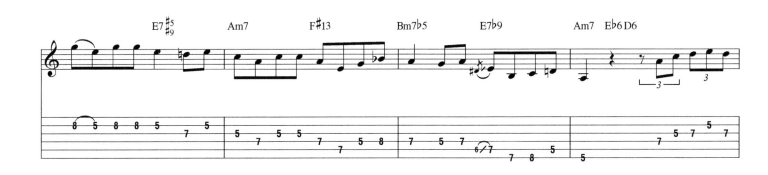

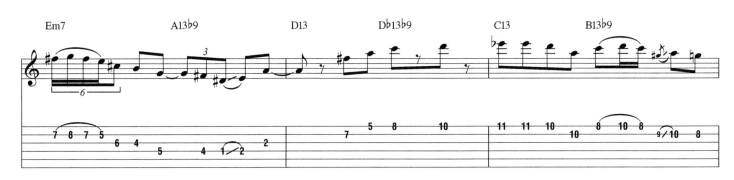

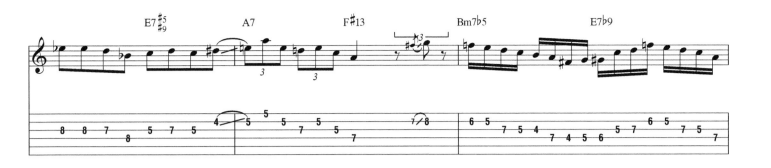

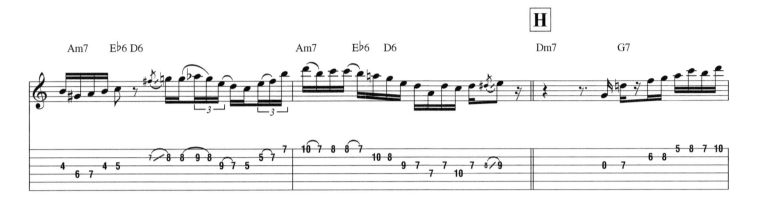

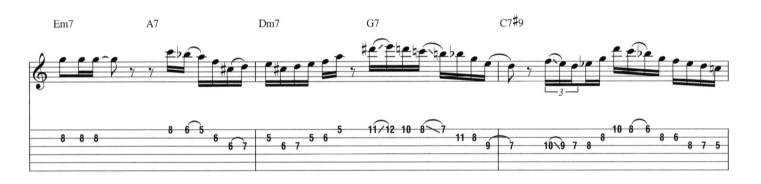

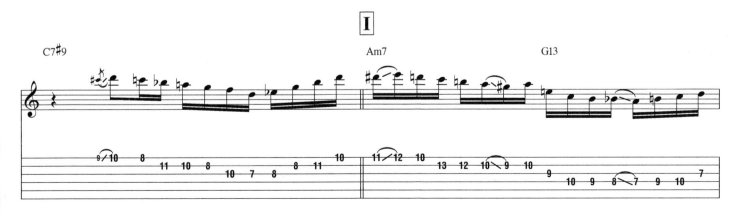

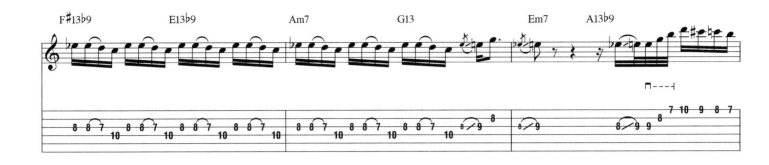

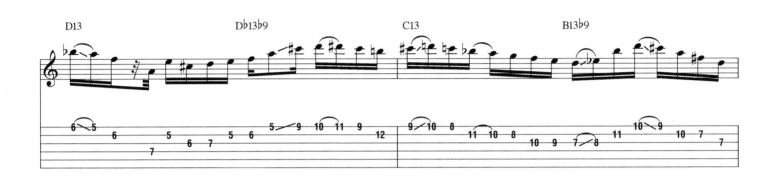

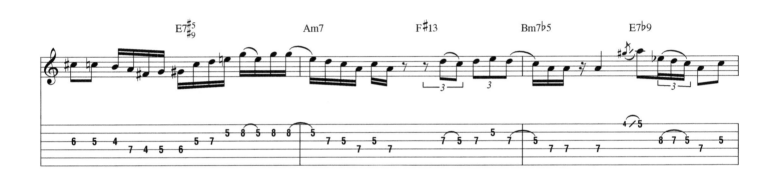

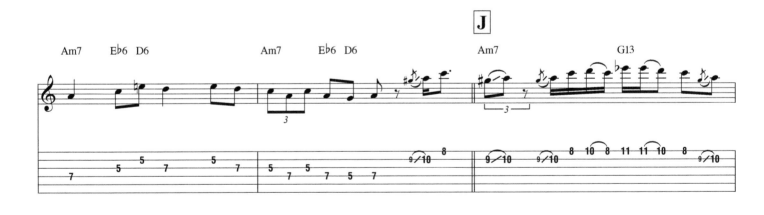

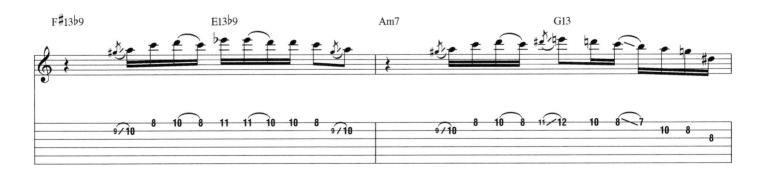

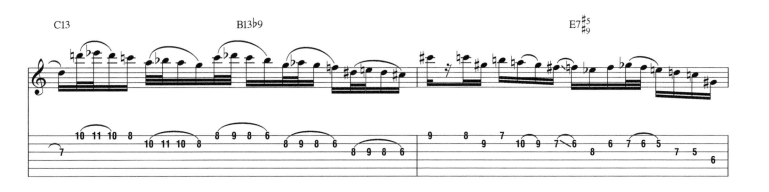

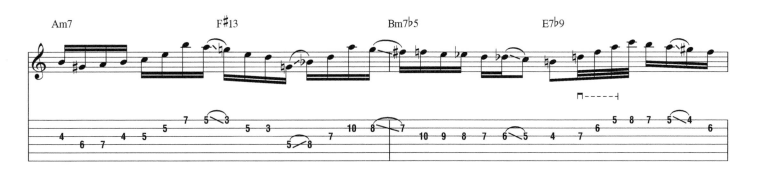

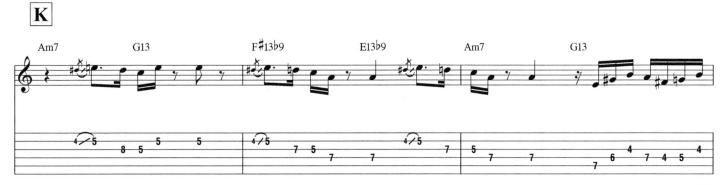

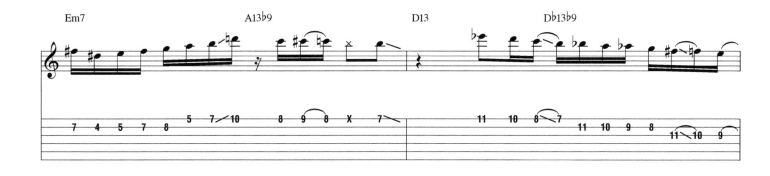

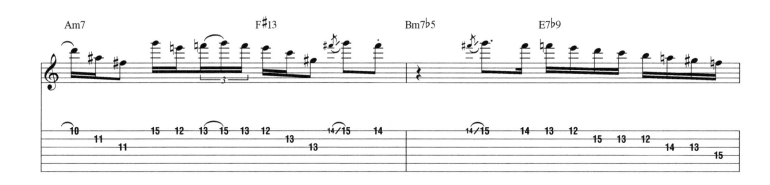

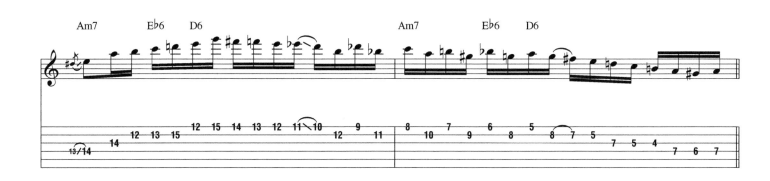

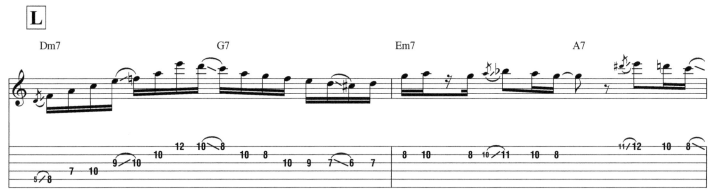

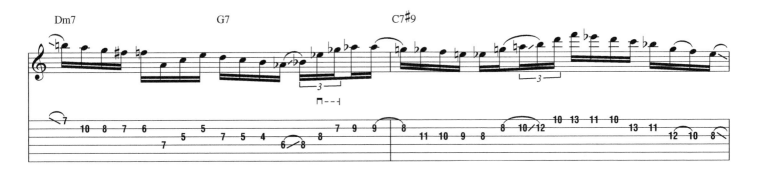

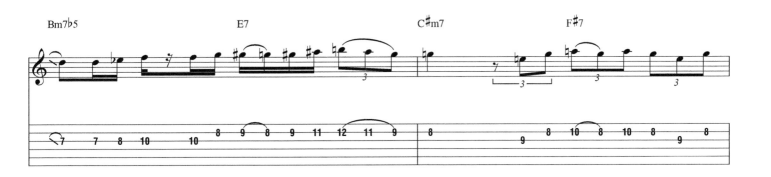

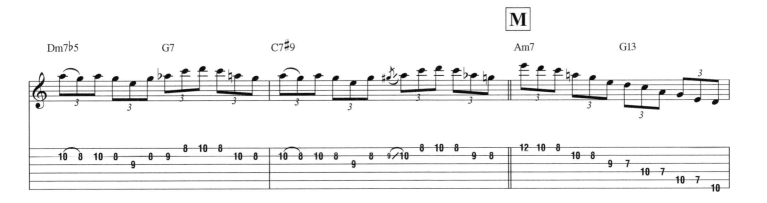

167

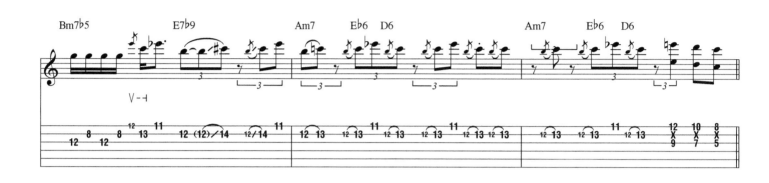

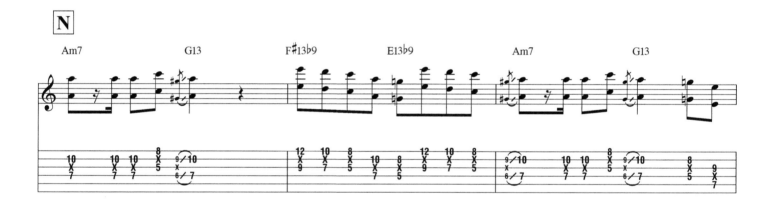

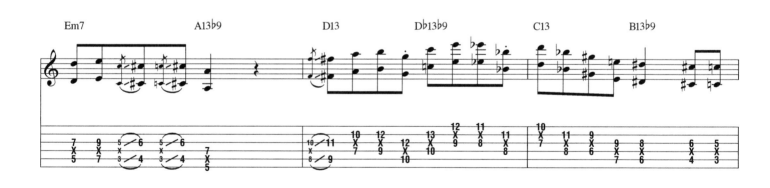

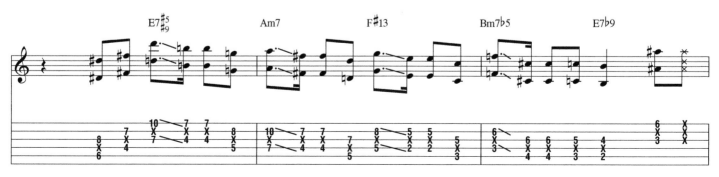

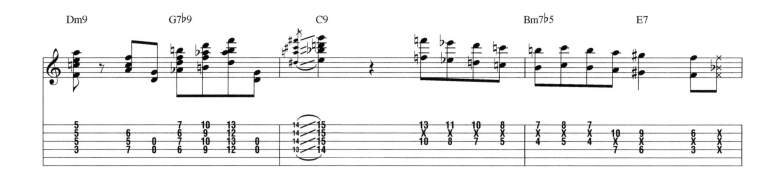

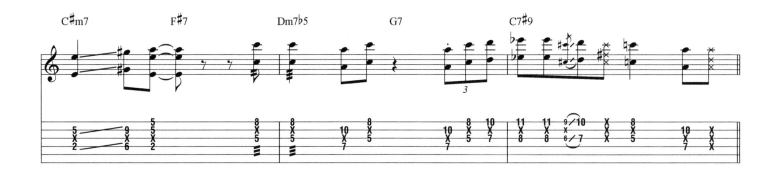

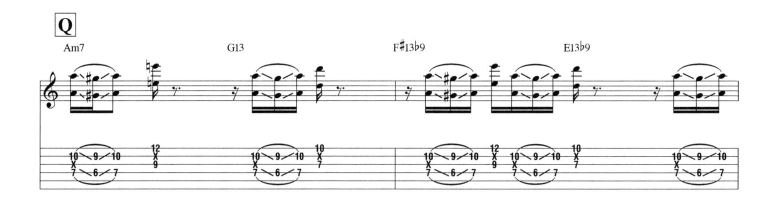

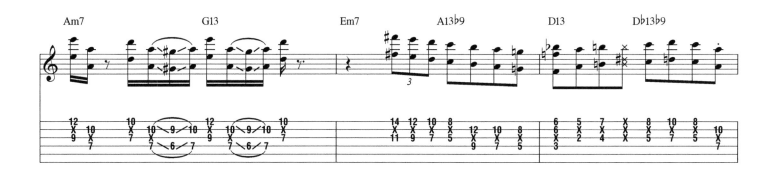

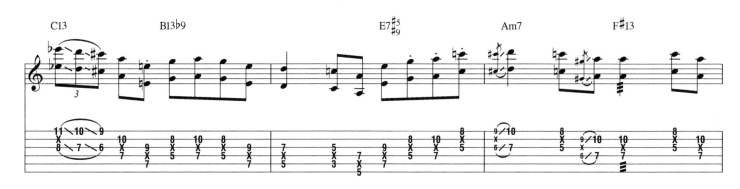

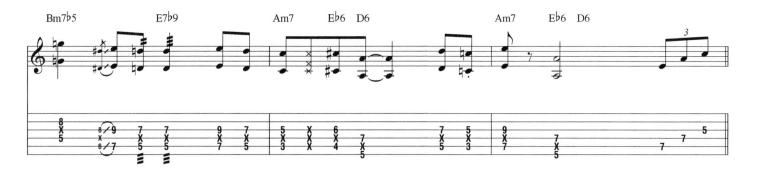

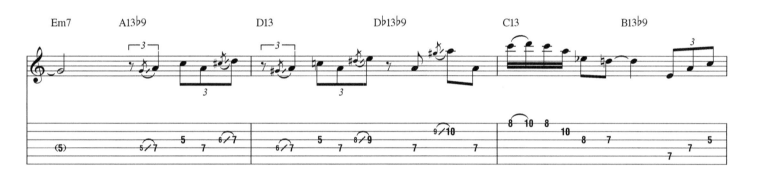

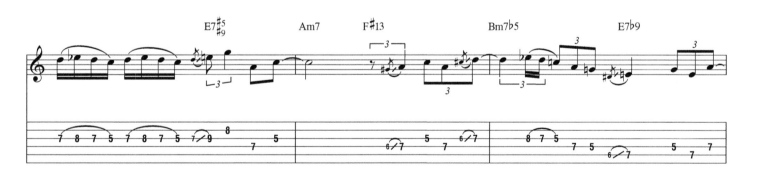

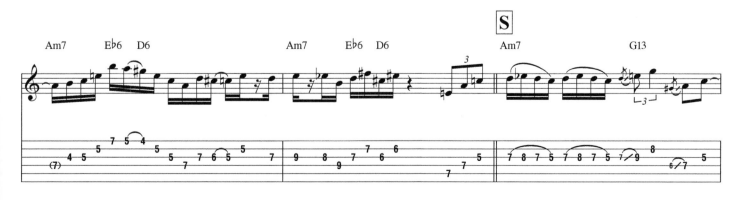

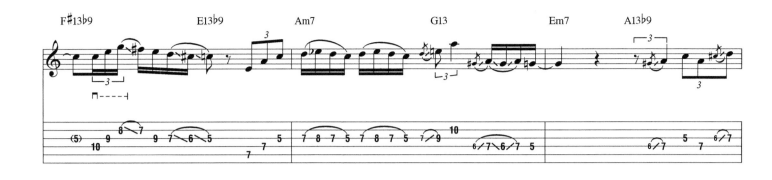

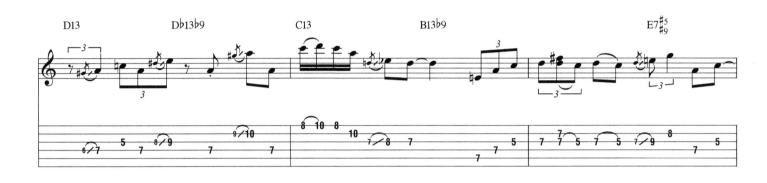

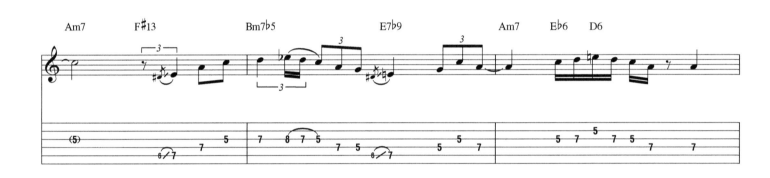

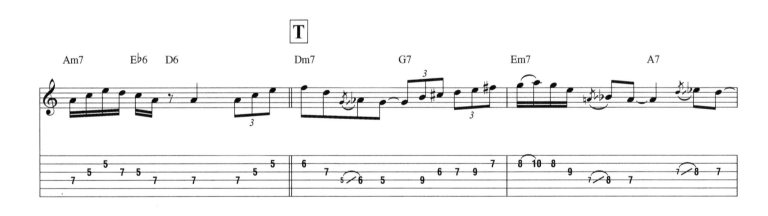

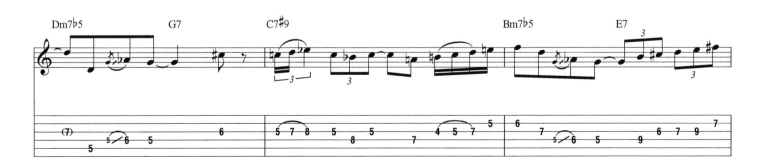

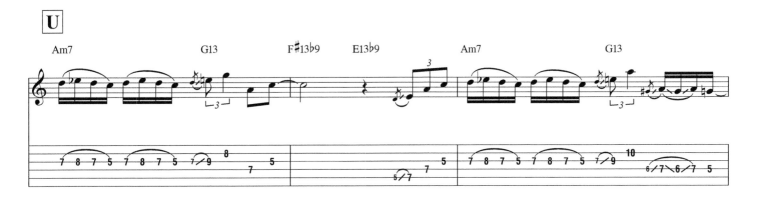

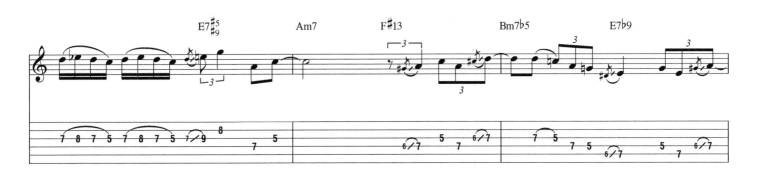

from *El Hombre*
Waltz for Geri
By Patrick Azzara

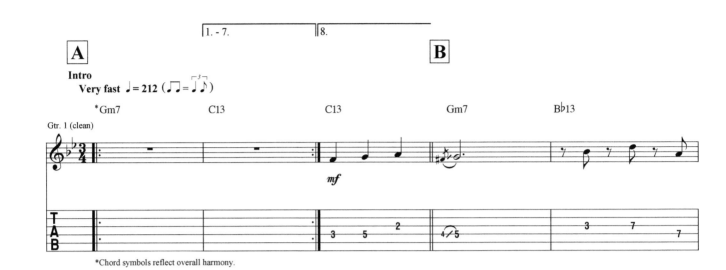

*Chord symbols reflect overall harmony.

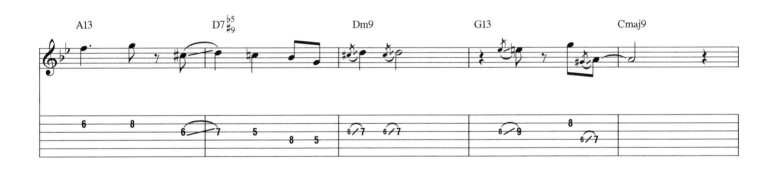

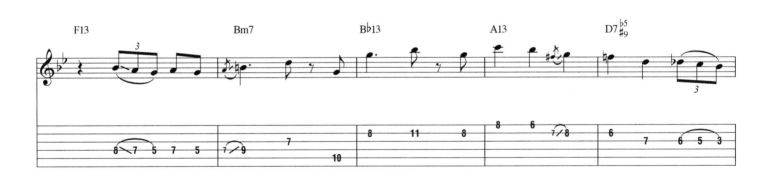

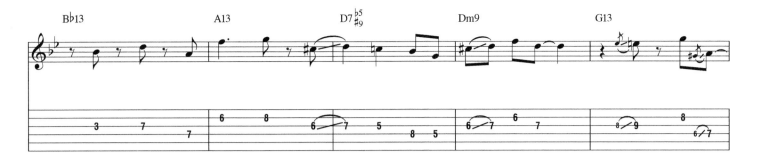

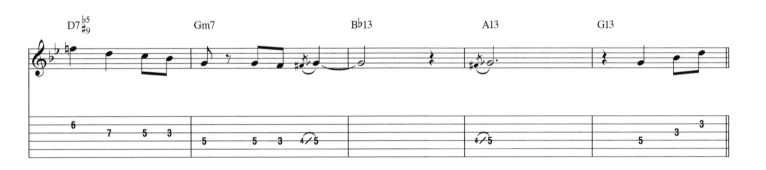

D

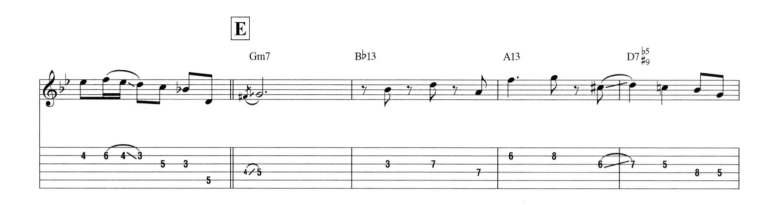

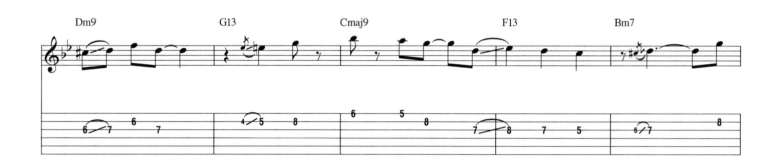

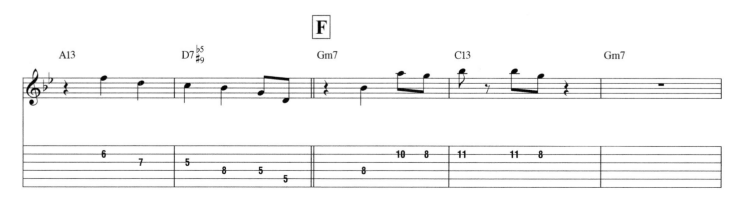

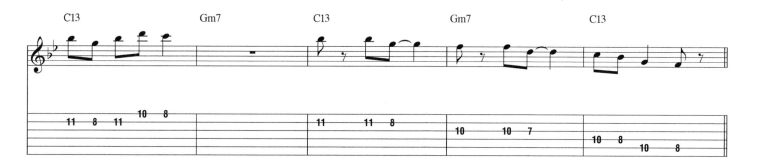

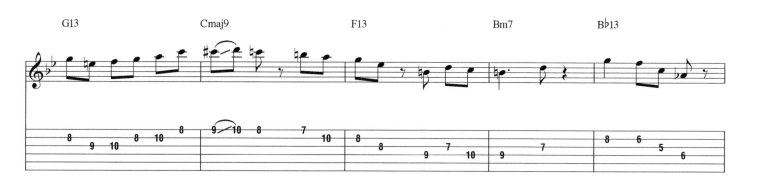

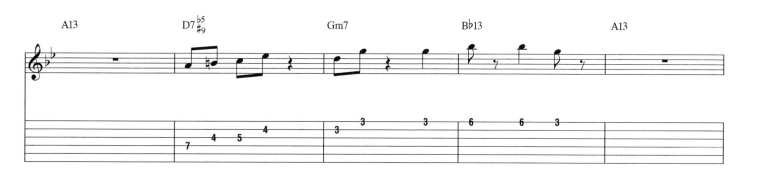

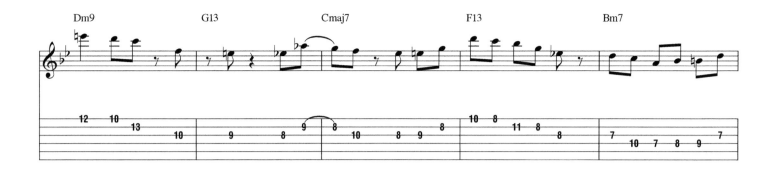

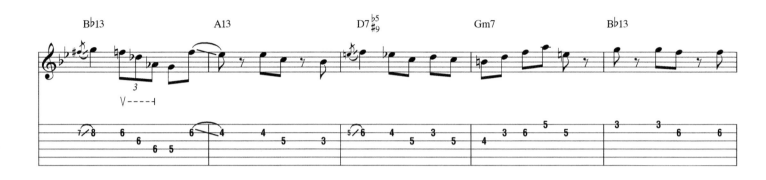

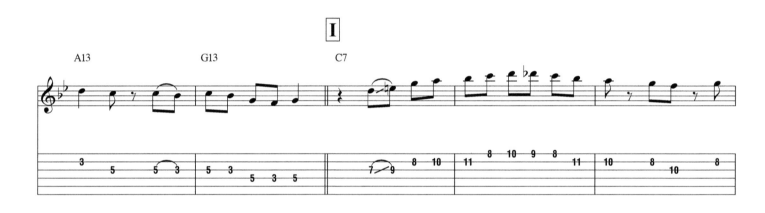

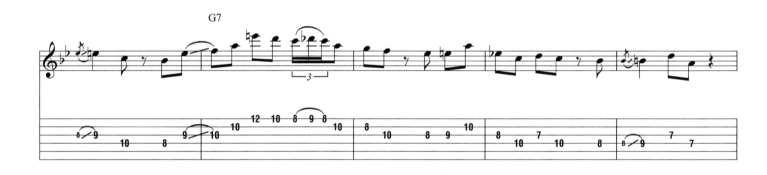

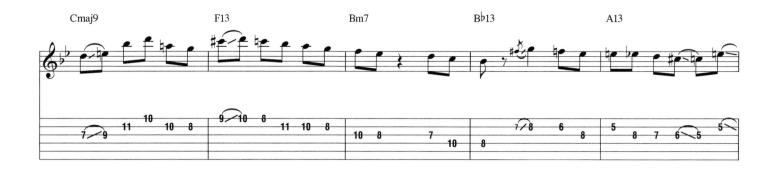

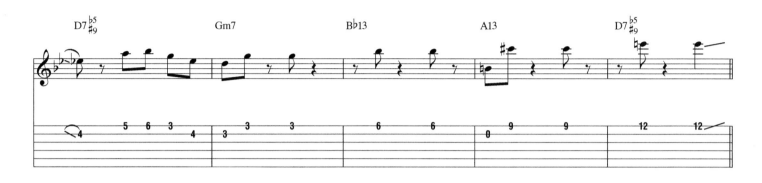

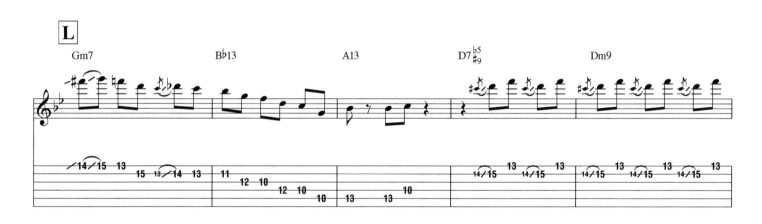

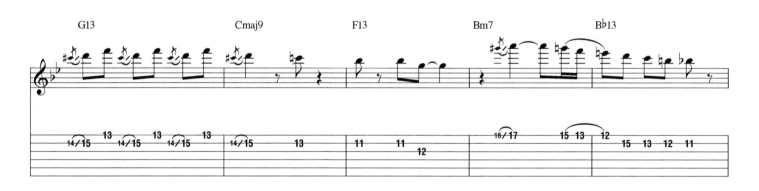

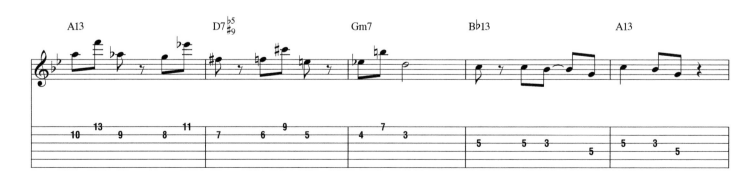

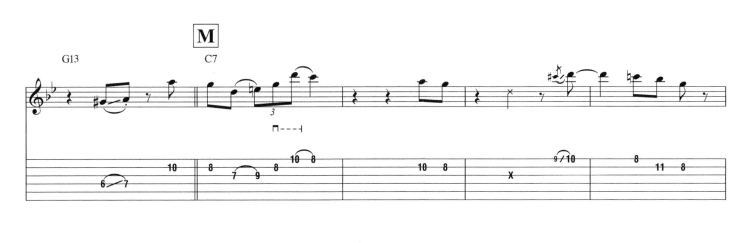

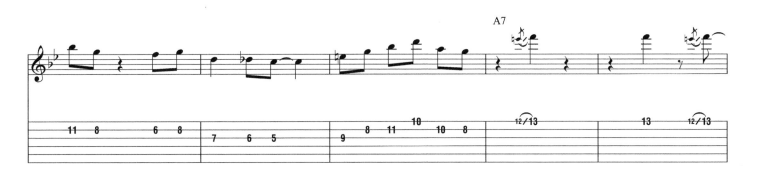

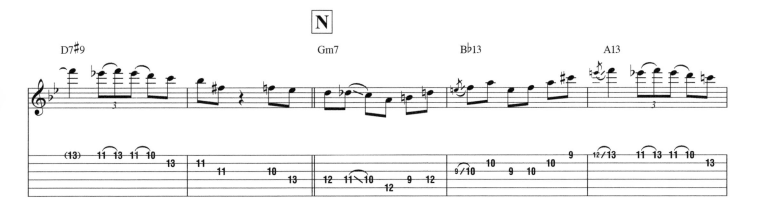

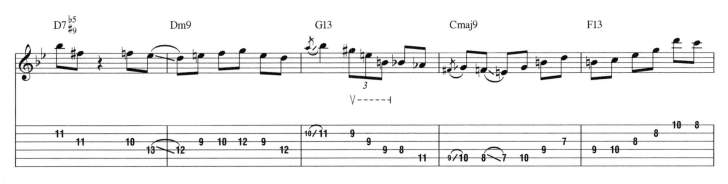

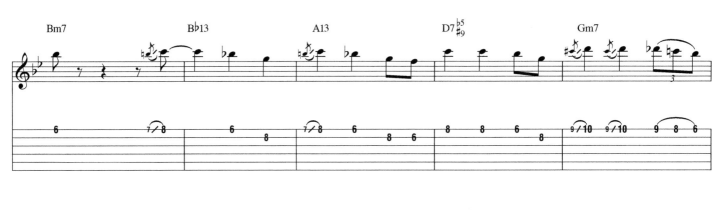

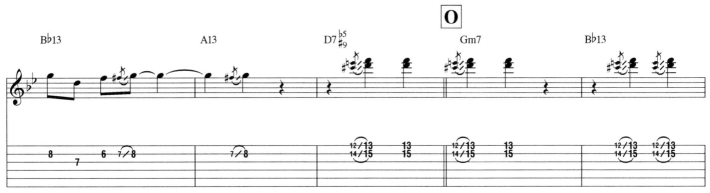

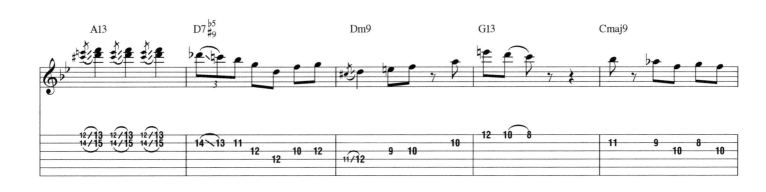

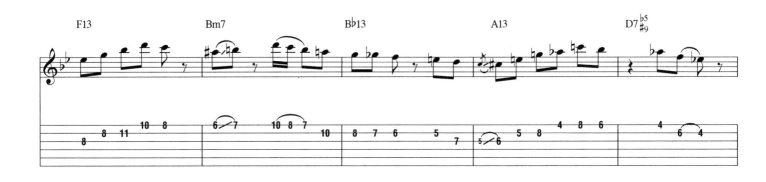

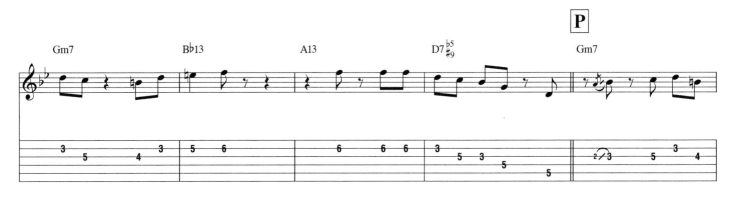

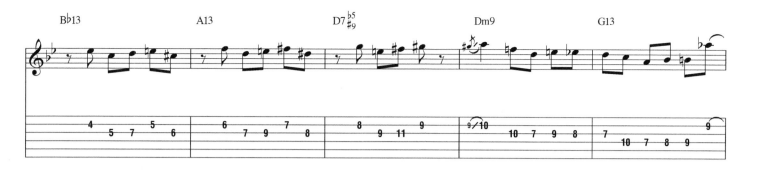

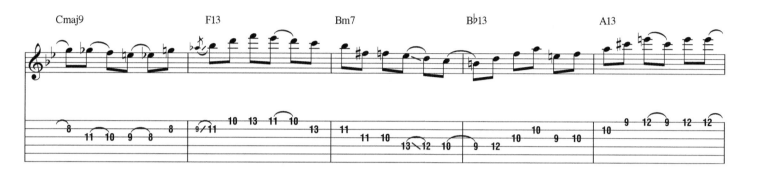

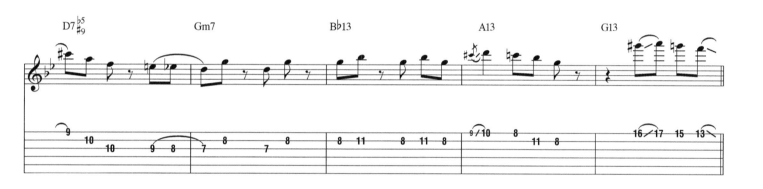

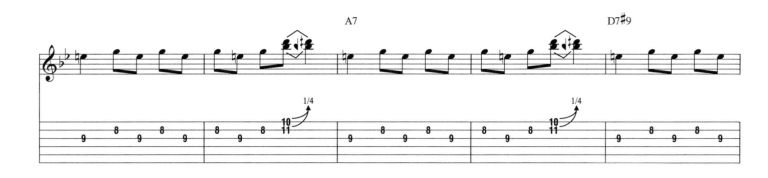

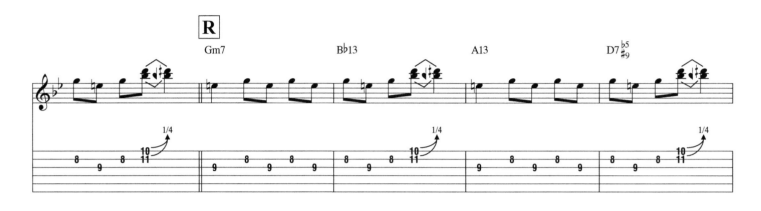

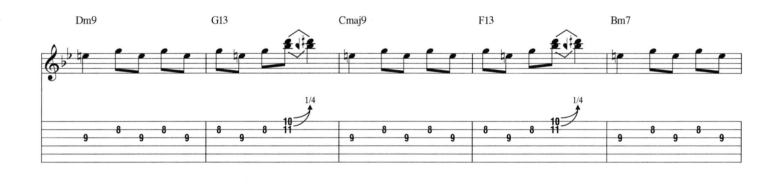

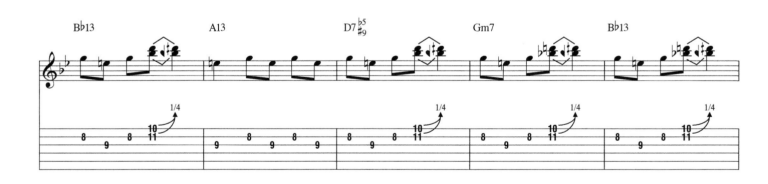

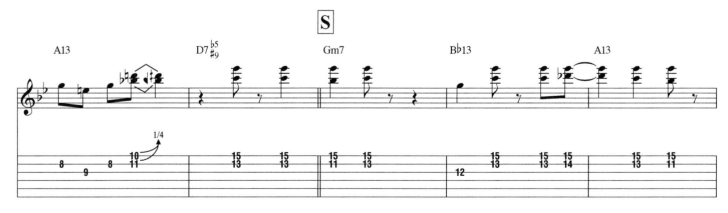

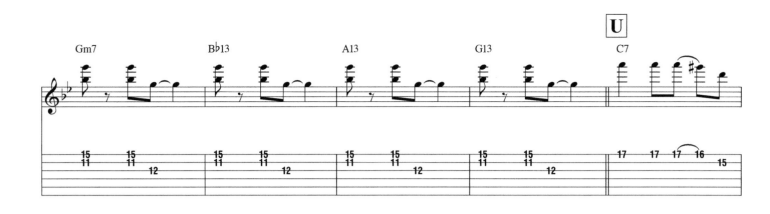

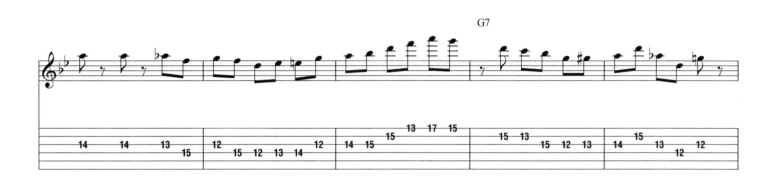

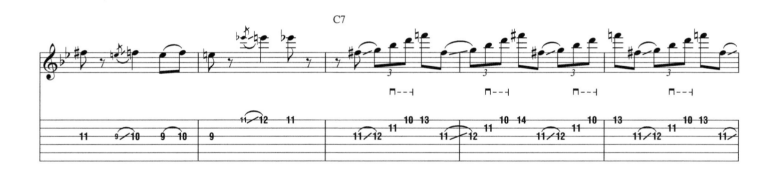

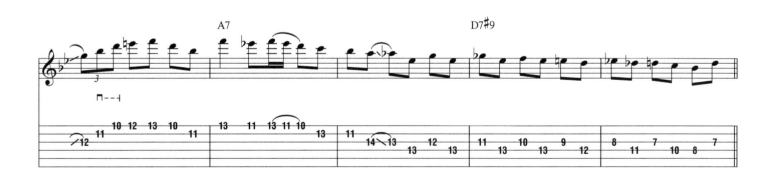

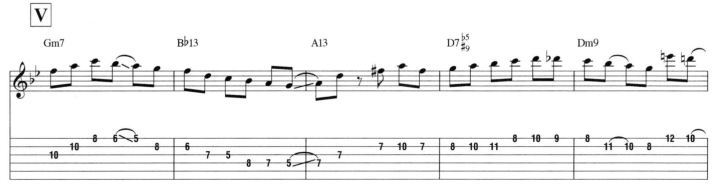

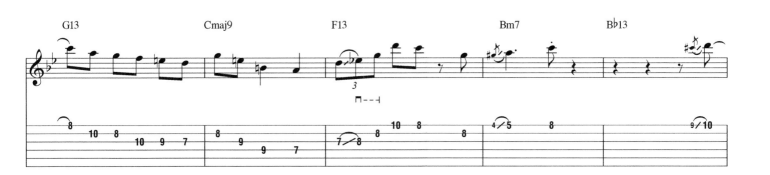

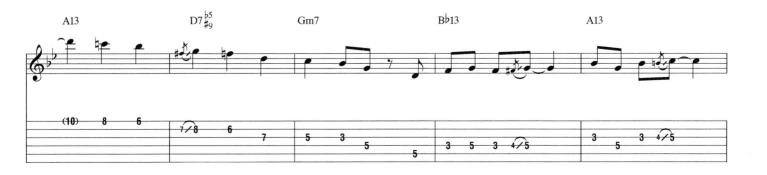

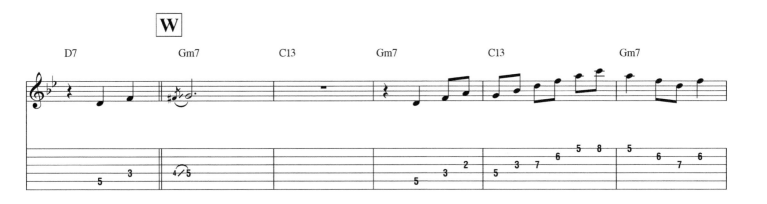

187

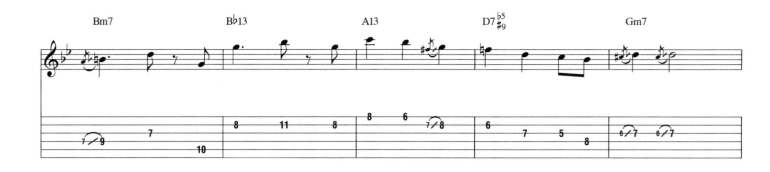

Y

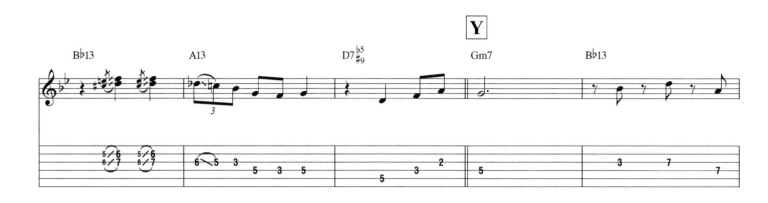

Z

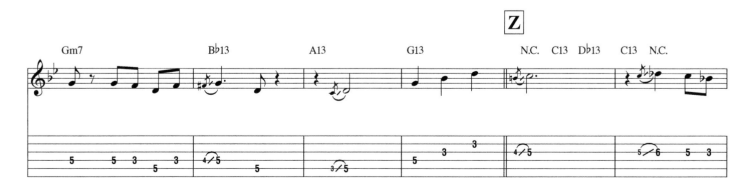

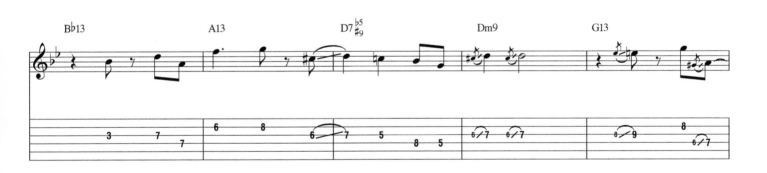

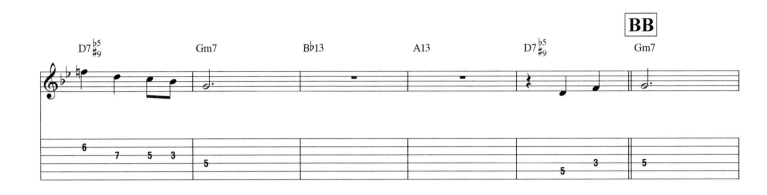

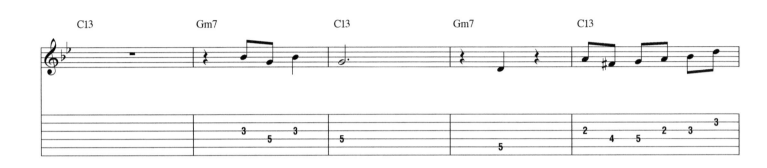

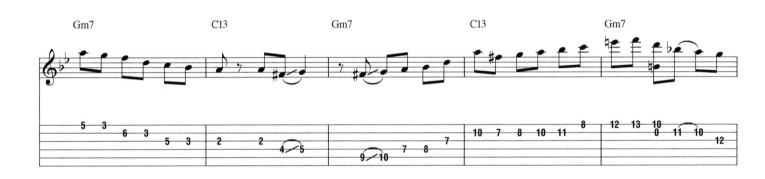

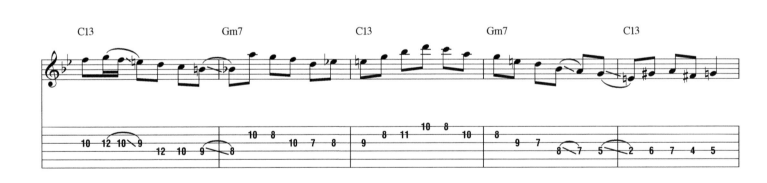

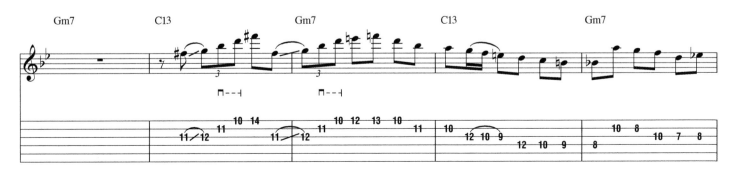

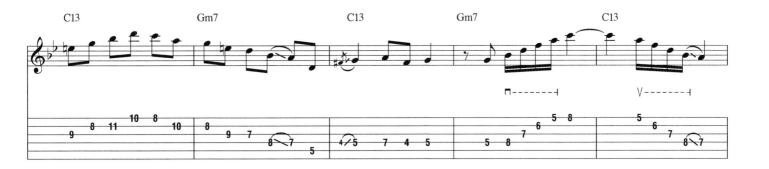

Begin fade

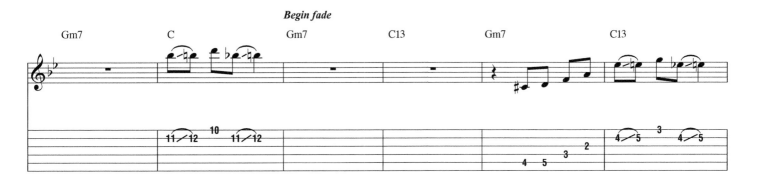

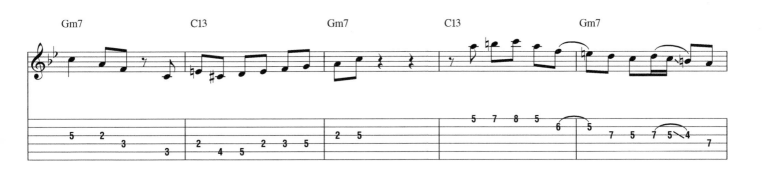

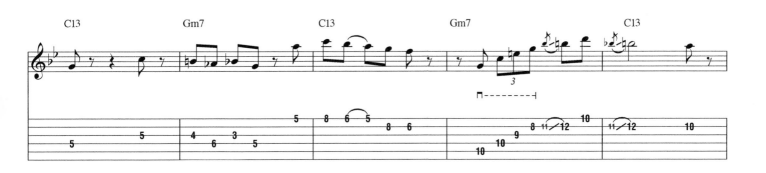

Fade out

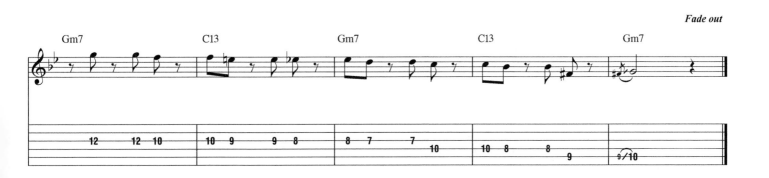

You Don't Know What Love Is

Words and Music by Don Raye and Gene DePaul

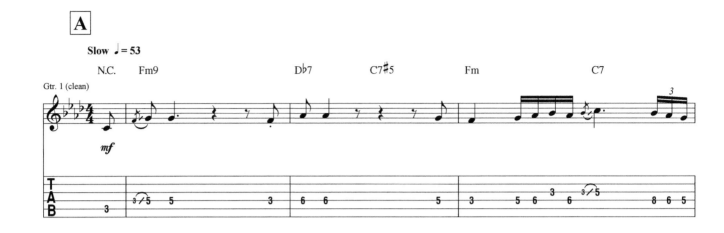

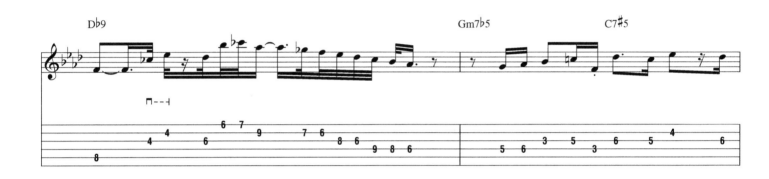

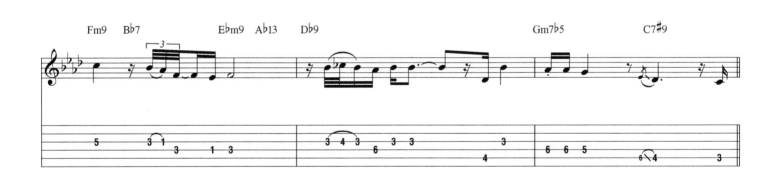

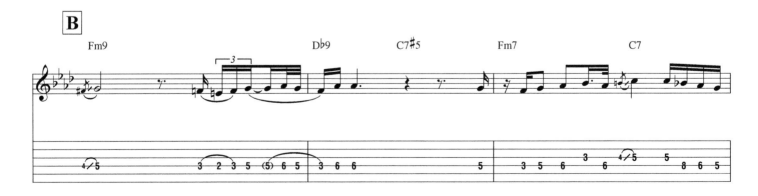

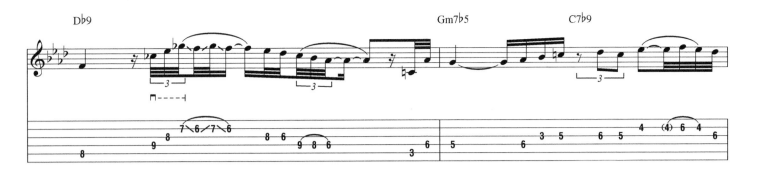

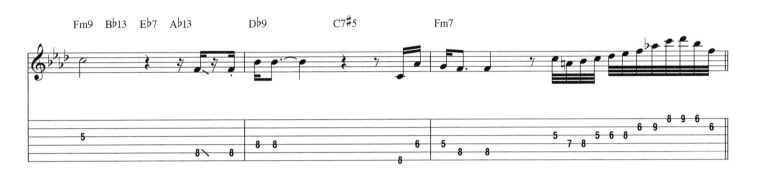

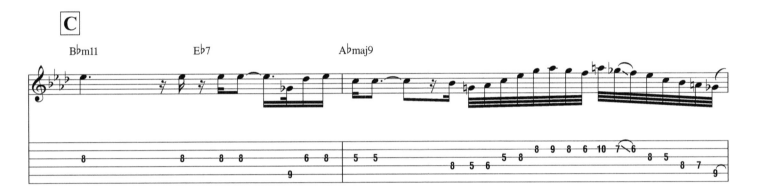

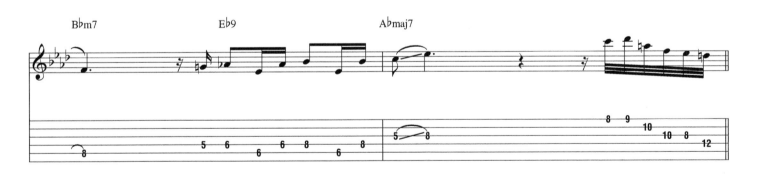

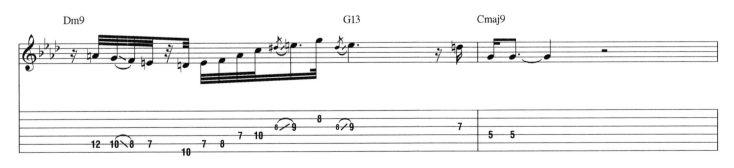

D

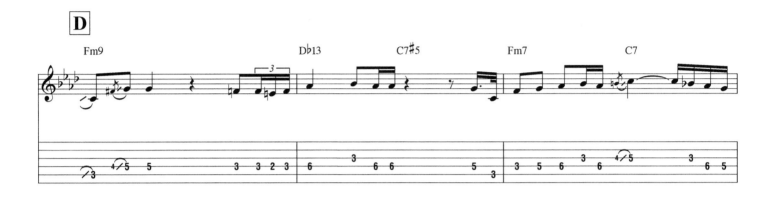

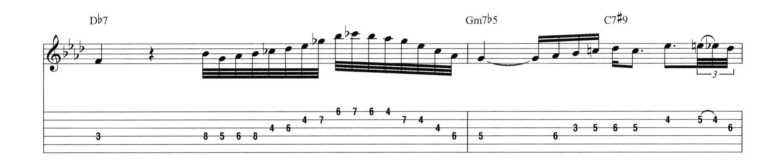

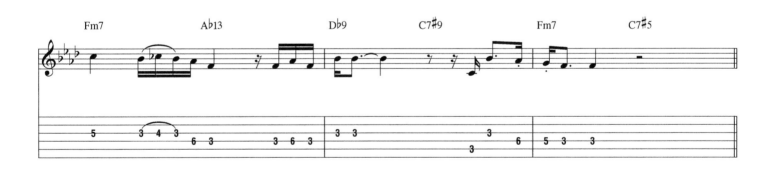

E

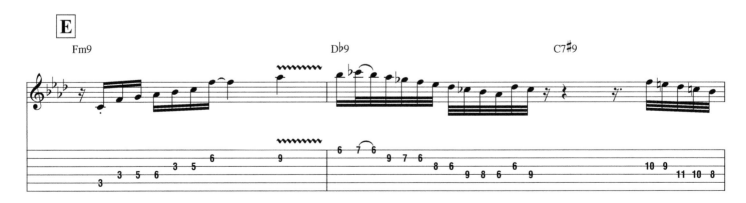

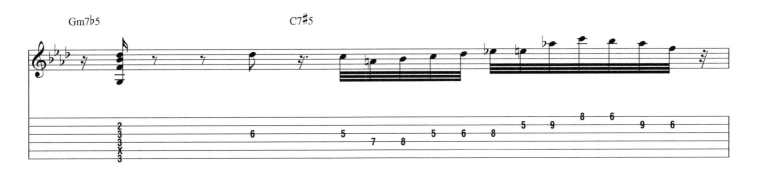

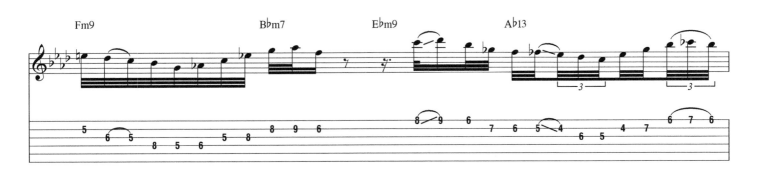

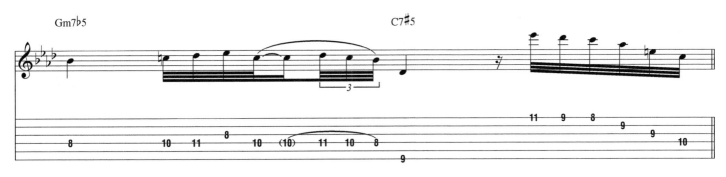

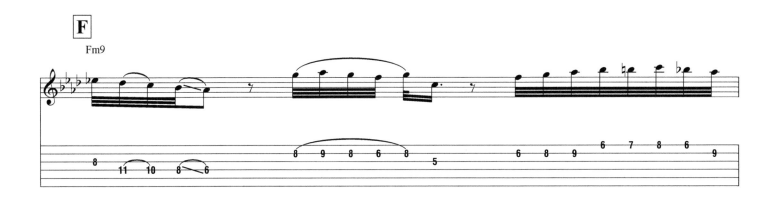

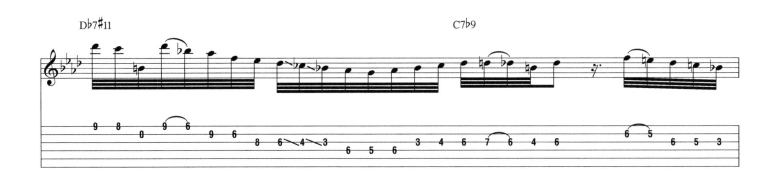

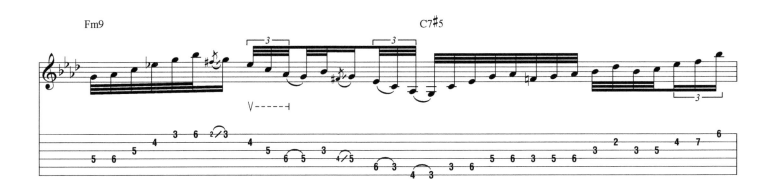

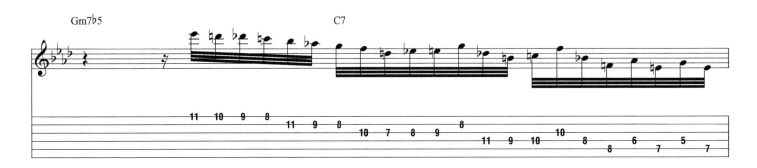

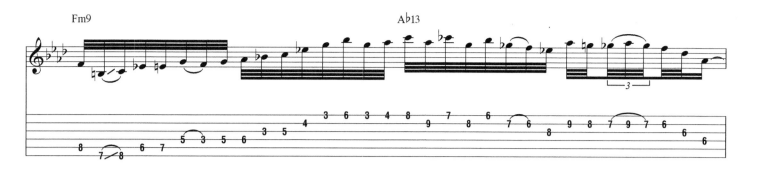

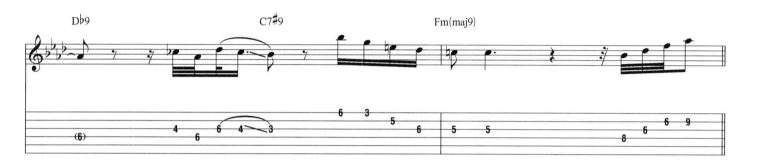

G

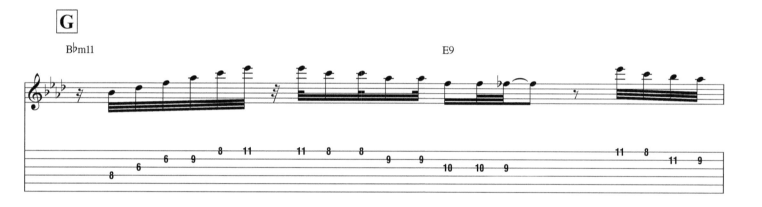

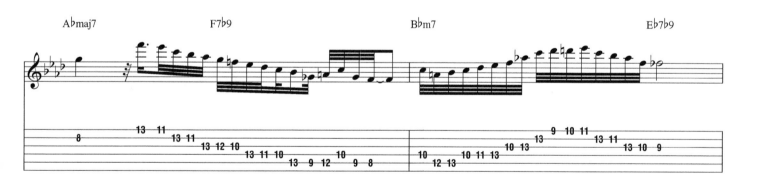

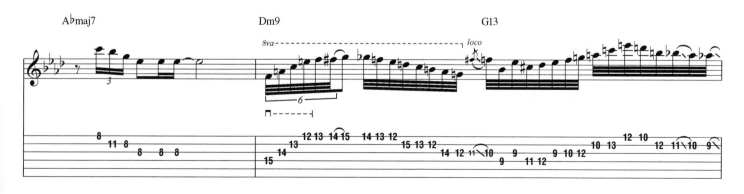

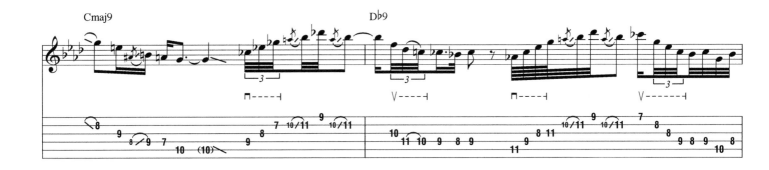

H

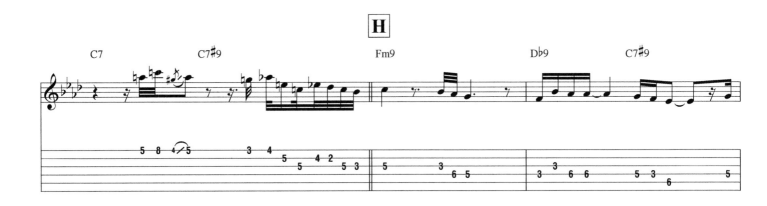

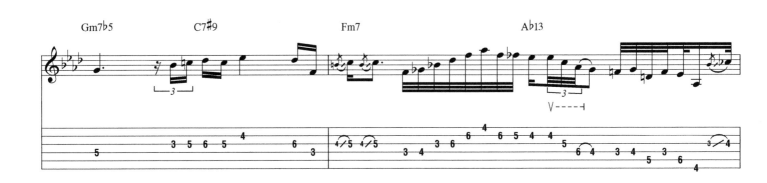

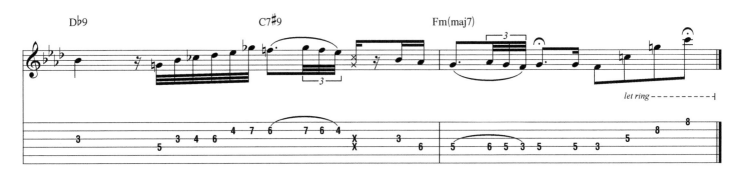

GUITAR NOTATION LEGEND

Guitar music can be notated three different ways: on a *musical staff*, in *tablature*, and in *rhythm slashes*.

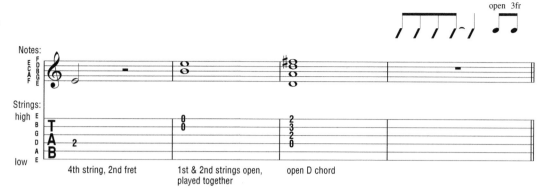

RHYTHM SLASHES are written above the staff. Strum chords in the rhythm indicated. Use the chord diagrams found at the top of the first page of the transcription for the appropriate chord voicings. Round noteheads indicate single notes.

THE MUSICAL STAFF shows pitches and rhythms and is divided by bar lines into measures. Pitches are named after the first seven letters of the alphabet.

TABLATURE graphically represents the guitar fingerboard. Each horizontal line represents a string, and each number represents a fret.

HALF-STEP BEND: Strike the note and bend up 1/2 step.

BEND AND RELEASE: Strike the note and bend up as indicated, then release back to the original note. Only the first note is struck.

HAMMER-ON: Strike the first (lower) note with one finger, then sound the higher note (on the same string) with another finger by fretting it without picking.

TRILL: Very rapidly alternate between the notes indicated by continuously hammering on and pulling off.

PICK SCRAPE: The edge of the pick is rubbed down (or up) the string, producing a scratchy sound.

TREMOLO PICKING: The note is picked as rapidly and continuously as possible.

WHOLE-STEP BEND: Strike the note and bend up one step.

PRE-BEND: Bend the note as indicated, then strike it.

PULL-OFF: Place both fingers on the notes to be sounded. Strike the first note and without picking, pull the finger off to sound the second (lower) note.

TAPPING: Hammer ("tap") the fret indicated with the pick-hand index or middle finger and pull off to the note fretted by the fret hand.

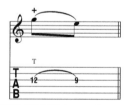

MUFFLED STRINGS: A percussive sound is produced by laying the fret hand across the string(s) without depressing, and striking them with the pick hand.

VIBRATO BAR DIVE AND RETURN: The pitch of the note or chord is dropped a specified number of steps (in rhythm), then returned to the original pitch.

GRACE NOTE BEND: Strike the note and immediately bend up as indicated.

VIBRATO: The string is vibrated by rapidly bending and releasing the note with the fretting hand.

LEGATO SLIDE: Strike the first note and then slide the same fret-hand finger up or down to the second note. The second note is not struck.

NATURAL HARMONIC: Strike the note while the fret-hand lightly touches the string directly over the fret indicated.

PALM MUTING: The note is partially muted by the pick hand lightly touching the string(s) just before the bridge.

VIBRATO BAR SCOOP: Depress the bar just before striking the note, then quickly release the bar.

SLIGHT (MICROTONE) BEND: Strike the note and bend up 1/4 step.

WIDE VIBRATO: The pitch is varied to a greater degree by vibrating with the fretting hand.

SHIFT SLIDE: Same as legato slide, except the second note is struck.

PINCH HARMONIC: The note is fretted normally and a harmonic is produced by adding the edge of the thumb or the tip of the index finger of the pick hand to the normal pick attack.

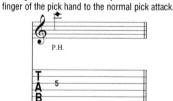

RAKE: Drag the pick across the strings indicated with a single motion.

VIBRATO BAR DIP: Strike the note and then immediately drop a specified number of steps, then release back to the original pitch.

The Best-Selling Jazz Book of All Time Is Now Legal!

The Real Books are the most popular jazz books of all time. Since the 1970s, musicians have trusted these volumes to get them through every gig, night after night. The problem is that the books were illegally produced and distributed, without any regard to copyright law, or royalties paid to the composers who created these musical masterpieces.

Hal Leonard is very proud to present the first legitimate and legal editions of these books ever produced. You won't even notice the difference, other than all the notorious errors being fixed: the covers and typeface look the same, the song lists are nearly identical, and the price for our edition is even cheaper than the originals!

Every conscientious musician will appreciate that these books are now produced accurately and ethically, benefitting the songwriters that we owe for some of the greatest tunes of all time!

VOLUME 1
00240221	C Edition	$39.99
00240224	Bb Edition	$39.99
00240225	Eb Edition	$39.99
00240226	Bass Clef Edition	$39.99
00286389	F Edition	$39.99
00240292	C Edition 6 x 9	$35.00
00240339	Bb Edition 6 x 9	$35.00
00147792	Bass Clef Edition 6 x 9	$35.00
00451087	C Edition on CD-ROM	$29.99
00200984	Online Backing Tracks: Selections	$45.00
00110604	Book/USB Flash Drive Backing Tracks Pack	$79.99
00110599	USB Flash Drive Only	$50.00

VOLUME 2
00240222	C Edition	$39.99
00240227	Bb Edition	$39.99
00240228	Eb Edition	$39.99
00240229	Bass Clef Edition	$39.99
00240293	C Edition 6 x 9	$35.00
00125900	Bb Edition 6 x 9	$35.00
00451088	C Edition on CD-ROM	$30.99
00125900	The Real Book – Mini Edition	$35.00
00204126	Backing Tracks on USB Flash Drive	$50.00
00204131	C Edition – USB Flash Drive Pack	$79.99

VOLUME 3
00240233	C Edition	$39.99
00240284	Bb Edition	$39.99
00240285	Eb Edition	$39.99
00240286	Bass Clef Edition	$39.99
00240338	C Edition 6 x 9	$35.00
00451089	C Edition on CD-ROM	$29.99

VOLUME 4
00240296	C Edition	$39.99
00103348	Bb Edition	$39.99
00103349	Eb Edition	$39.99
00103350	Bass Clef Edition	$39.99

VOLUME 5
00240349	C Edition	$39.99
00175278	Bb Edition	$39.99
00175279	Eb Edition	$39.99

VOLUME 6
00240534	C Edition	$39.99
00223637	Eb Edition	$39.99

Also available:
00154230	The Real Bebop Book	$34.99
00240264	The Real Blues Book	$34.99
00310910	The Real Bluegrass Book	$35.00
00240223	The Real Broadway Book	$35.00
00240440	The Trane Book	$22.99
00125426	The Real Country Book	$39.99
00269721	The Real Miles Davis Book C Edition	$24.99
00269723	The Real Miles Davis Book Bb Edition	$24.99
00240355	The Real Dixieland Book C Edition	$32.50
00294853	The Real Dixieland Book Eb Edition	$35.00
00122335	The Real Dixieland Book Bb Edition	$35.00
00240235	The Duke Ellington Real Book	$22.99
00240268	The Real Jazz Solos Book	$30.00
00240348	The Real Latin Book C Edition	$37.50
00127107	The Real Latin Book Bb Edition	$35.00
00120809	The Pat Metheny Real Book C Edition	$27.50
00252119	The Pat Metheny Real Book Bb Edition	$24.99
00240358	The Charlie Parker Real Book C Edition	$19.99
00275997	The Charlie Parker Real Book Eb Edition	$19.99
00118324	The Real Pop Book – Vol. 1	$35.00
00240331	The Bud Powell Real Book	$19.99
00240437	The Real R&B Book C Edition	$39.99
00276590	The Real R&B Book Bb Edition	$39.99
00240313	The Real Rock Book	$35.00
00240323	The Real Rock Book – Vol. 2	$35.00
00240359	The Real Tab Book	$32.50
00240317	The Real Worship Book	$29.99

THE REAL CHRISTMAS BOOK
00240306	C Edition	$32.50
00240345	Bb Edition	$32.50
00240346	Eb Edition	$35.00
00240347	Bass Clef Edition	$32.50
00240431	A-G CD Backing Tracks	$24.99
00240432	H-M CD Backing Tracks	$24.99
00240433	N-Y CD Backing Tracks	$24.99

THE REAL VOCAL BOOK
00240230	Volume 1 High Voice	$35.00
00240307	Volume 1 Low Voice	$35.00
00240231	Volume 2 High Voice	$35.00
00240308	Volume 2 Low Voice	$35.00
00240391	Volume 3 High Voice	$35.00
00240392	Volume 3 Low Voice	$35.00
00118318	Volume 4 High Voice	$35.00
00118319	Volume 4 Low Voice	$35.00

Complete song lists online at www.halleonard.com